LESSONS FOR
FIRST GRADE

THE TEACHING ARITHMETIC SERIES

Teaching
ARITHMETIC

LESSONS FOR
FIRST GRADE

▲▲▲▲▲

STEPHANIE SHEFFIELD

MATH SOLUTIONS PUBLICATIONS
SAUSALITO, CA

Math Solutions Publications
A division of
Marilyn Burns Education Associates
150 Gate 5 Road, Suite 101
Sausalito, CA 94965
www.mathsolutions.com

Library of Congress Cataloging-in-Publication Data
Sheffield, Stephanie.
    Teaching arithmetic : lessons for first grade / Stephanie Sheffield.
        p. cm.
Includes index.
    ISBN 0-941355-34-9
    1. Arithmetic—Study and teaching (Primary)   I. Title.
QA135.6 .S48 2001
    372.7—dc21
                                                                    2001003778

Editor: Toby Gordon
Production: Melissa L. Inglis
Cover & interior design: Leslie Bauman
Composition: Argosy Publishing

Printed in the United States of America on acid-free paper
05 04 03 02 01   ML   1 2 3 4 5

A Message from Marilyn Burns

We at Marilyn Burns Education Associates believe that teaching mathematics well calls for continually reflecting on and improving one s instructional practice. Our Math Solutions Publications include a wide range of choices, from books in our new Teaching Arithmetic series which address beginning number concepts, place value, addition, subtraction, multiplication, division, fractions, decimals, and percents to resources that help link math with writing and literature; from books that help teachers more deeply understand the mathematics behind the math they teach to children s books that help students develop an appreciation for math while learning basic concepts.

Along with our large collection of teacher resource books, we have a more general collection of books, videotapes, and audiotapes that can help teachers and parents bridge the gap between home and school. All of our materials are available at education stores, from distributors, and through major teacher catalogs.

In addition, Math Solutions Inservice offers five-day courses and one-day workshops throughout the country. We also work in partnership with school districts to help implement and sustain long-term improvement in mathematics instruction in all classrooms.

To find a complete listing of our publications and workshops, please visit our Web site at *www.mathsolutions.com*. Or contact us by calling (800) 868-9092 or sending an e-mail to *info@mathsolutions.com*.

We re eager for your feedback and interested in learning about your particular needs. We look forward to hearing from you.

A DIVISION OF MARILYN BURNS EDUCATION ASSOCIATES

CONTENTS

ACKNOWLEDGMENTS

Special thanks to Sheri Dittert, Jan Fariss, Mary Karnick, Maggie Lopez, and Sherri Trammell for teaching lessons in their classrooms and sharing their expertise with me.

Special thanks for help and encouragement to Marilyn Burns, without whose inspiration I would never have written; Toby Gordon, for her patience and encouragement, and for the gentle but persistent nagging; and Melissa Inglis for cheerfully seeing this book through publication.

Special thanks also to Shellie Liles, whose leadership as principal creates a school climate that encourages creative teaching; the teachers, children, and staff of Beneke Elementary School, who together make school a fun place to be every day; Mary Karnick, my first-grade teaching partner for two years, whose love of first graders and sense of humor helped make me a better teacher, and whose friendship sustained me through the rough spots; and Karen Economoupolos for many long conversations and for reading each lesson—I value her thoughtful consideration and deep understanding of children's learning as much as her friendship.

And last, but not least, special thanks to Katharine, Caren, Rusty, Rita, Lisa, Becky, Claire, and Mom, for all the times you reminded me that I could do it; and my family, Carl, Megan, and Patrick, for bearing with me, and helping in every way.

INTRODUCTION

I remember that in first grade, the subject on my report card right under reading was arithmetic. In my life at that time, arithmetic meant learning my facts—and trying to be fast with them—and mastering procedures for adding and subtracting. What I learned about arithmetic was that if you followed the rules and put the right numbers in the right places, you got the answers right.

To be truthful, arithmetic never made much sense to me. In fact, it never occurred to me that the facts I learned and the algorithms I performed were supposed to make sense. And so, instead of being a meaningful tool that I could use to solve problems and learn more about the world around me, arithmetic was a subject to be endured in school.

Even later, when the subject on my report card changed from arithmetic to mathematics, my teachers still taught in the same way. I learned the times tables and more algorithms for adding, subtracting, multiplying, and dividing, working first with large whole numbers and later with fractions, decimals, and percents. Even more than before, my understanding was limited to the rules and the procedures that I memorized. It never occurred to me that what I was learning was somehow useful beyond passing quizzes and tests, and it certainly never occurred to me that doing mathematics could be fun.

I'm saddened by what I experienced as an elementary student. But my experience has, in an important way, served me well in my teaching. It convinced me that I wanted to provide a different experience for my students, to provide them the chance both to learn more and to enjoy what they were learning.

At some point in my teaching career, I became a student of mathematics again. I relearned familiar mathematics concepts and skills, finally understanding them, and learned other mathematics concepts and skills for the first time. I discovered that, in fact, mathematics could make sense and could be interesting. I now found mathematics intriguing enough to even call it fun!

Arithmetic Teaching Today

One of the biggest shifts that I've seen in my twenty years of teaching is that we have broadened our definition of mathematics learning for elementary children. We now see elementary mathematics in a context larger than arithmetic. Of course, arithmetic is still important; it's a tool for solving problems, an essential life skill. But we now know that children need the knowledge and the confidence to make sense of problems in all areas of mathematics as well as to learn how and when to apply computation skills accurately and efficiently to find solutions.

That said, just as I spent a good deal of time learning arithmetic in first grade, arithmetic remains the primary focus of my students' math learning. However, because of the vision that I now hold in my mind of arithmetic as part of the larger study of mathematics, the learning experiences I provide are very different from what I remember experiencing as a first grader.

Goals for First-Grade Arithmetic Instruction

Children come to school with a good deal of mathematical knowledge. Most of them know how to count, and they know that numbers can be used to describe quantities or to represent something like a telephone number or a shoe size. They've encountered many situations that call for combining, separating, and sharing quantities. Also, most first graders come into the classroom on the first day of school excited and expecting to learn something new. It seems only natural in first grade to build on children's interest in numbers.

My arithmetic program is based on addressing three areas: computation, problem solving, and number sense. Each of these is essential to arithmetic learning and together they provide the structure for the arithmetic instruction I offer first graders. The categories are not separate and unrelated but rather are deeply intertwined. Each one relies on and supports the other two. When solving problems, for example, students must apply their computation skills to figure out answers and also rely on their number sense to decide if their answers are reasonable given the context and the numbers involved. When computing, children rely on the problem context to identify the numbers to use and on their number sense to choose appropriate approaches and evaluate their answers. And developing number sense is key for helping children develop numerical knowledge and see how numbers relate to one another, skills necessary for both computation and problem solving.

I try to keep all three categories in mind as I plan arithmetic lessons. The mix of computation, number sense, and problem-solving experiences guides my students in learning how numbers are structured in our number system, understanding relationships among numbers, and developing skills for adding and subtracting. From their experiences, children come to see that understanding numbers and how they work, and applying skills to problem-solving situations, is as important to learn as the skills for addition and subtraction.

I also have other goals for first graders. I want my students to see the usefulness of arithmetic for solving real problems that arise in the classroom, as well as problems that emerge from the literature we read or situations that we create. I want my students to see themselves as mathematical thinkers. As they encounter and work through problems, I want them to develop the understanding that problems can be solved in many ways and that they have at their disposal valuable strategies for doing this. The characteristics of persistence and perseverance they learn in first grade will serve them throughout their later math learning.

Thoughts About Organizing the Year

Beginning a mathematical year in first grade is an exciting challenge. When setting up my classroom each year, I look for ways to make children feel comfortable. Children benefit from having other students close by to talk and work with, so I group their individual desks to allow them to sit in threes, fours, and fives. I also move desks as needed so that at times pairs of children or larger groups can work together. And I'm careful to arrange the desks so that all the children can easily see the chalkboard by turning their heads.

I establish in the classroom a large meeting area where the entire class can gather, and I use an easel with a white board for recording our work. Also, I set up several small areas around the room where children can go to play a game or work on a problem.

When working on problems, not only are the children free to choose the materials they wish to use, but I expect them to make their own choices. While there are times when I choose particular materials for a lesson, more often, when students have a problem to solve, they choose the tools to use. In this way, they have control over their own learning and can use materials that make sense to them.

To this end, I make sure that materials are easily accessible to my students. I store all of the math manipulatives in cabinets on low shelves so that children can reach them easily. As I introduce new manipulatives, I show the class where to find them and how to return them. For the manipulatives that we use often—interlocking cubes, playing cards, dice, and counters—I divide them up into smaller containers so that one or two students can quickly get just what they need. I keep paper in trays at the front of the room and a supply of clipboards available in a box where children can reach them whenever they choose to work on the floor.

Like many teachers, I teach a curriculum that is defined by objectives and expectations from the state and the school district. My school district provides a curriculum guide as well as a textbook, and these outline what I am required to teach. However, when planning instruction, I've found that there is no single book or program that provides all of the help I need to meet the learning needs of my first graders. As most teachers do, I use a collection of resources to meet these goals. I look for children's books, teacher-directed lessons, games, explorations, and homework assignments that can help my students interact with each concept they study in a variety of ways.

Each year the instructional choices I make vary. That's because every class has different temperaments, interests, and abilities, and these differences help guide my choices. Some classes need more time with a particular mathematical topic than others. Some classes become fascinated with a particular game or type of problem. Although these situations help guide my decisions about the year, the big mathematical ideas remain at the heart of my decisions. In the end, my choices are not about the games, the children's literature, or the specific activities, but rather about the math learning goals. And I'm constantly on the lookout for new and effective teaching ideas.

The Structure of the Lessons

In order to help you with planning and teaching the lessons in this book, each is presented in the same format with the following sections:

Overview   To help you decide if the lesson is appropriate for your students, this is a nutshell description of the mathematical goal of the lesson and what the students will be doing.

Materials   This section lists the special materials needed along with quantities. Not included in the list are regular classroom supplies such as pencils and paper. Worksheets that need to be duplicated are included in the Blackline Masters section at the back of the book.

Time   Generally, the number of class periods is provided, sometimes with a range allowing for different-length periods. It is also indicated for some activities that they are meant to be repeated from time to time.

Teaching Directions   The directions are presented in a step-by-step lesson plan.

Teaching Notes   This section addresses the mathematics underlying the lesson and at times provides information about the prior experiences or knowledge students need.

The Lesson   This is a vignette that describes what actually occurred when the lesson was taught to one or more classes. While the vignette mirrors the plan described in the teaching directions, it elaborates with details that are valuable for preparing and teaching the lesson. Samples of student work are included.

Extensions   This section is included for some of the lessons and offers follow-up suggestions.

Questions and Discussion   Presented in a question-and-answer format, this section addresses issues that came up during the lesson and/or have been posed by other teachers.

While organized similarly, the lessons here vary in several ways. Some span one class period, others take longer, and some are suitable to repeat over and over, giving children a chance to revisit ideas and extend their learning. Some use manipulative materials, others ask students to draw pictures, and others ask students to rely on reasoning mentally. And while some lessons seem to be more suited for beginning experiences, at times it's beneficial for more experienced students to engage with them as well. An activity that seems simple can reinforce students' understanding or give them a fresh way to look at a familiar concept. Also, a lesson that initially seems too difficult or advanced can be ideal for introducing students to thinking in a new way.

How to Use This Book

This collection of lessons is not intended to be a complete arithmetic curriculum. Rather, I chose the lessons in this book because they engaged my students, challenged them, and helped grow their mathematical thinking. Each has been tried in several first-grade classes and polished over time. To teach all of the lessons as described in the sixteen chapters requires more than thirty class periods, not including time for daily routines to incorporate into your yearlong instruction, for repeat experiences as recommended for some lessons, or for the assessment ideas suggested at the end of the book.

The first section in the book presents four introductory lessons that are appropriate for the beginning of the year. These lessons help build a classroom culture for learning arithmetic that is useful in all of the subsequent lessons. The first lesson focuses on building the calendar and establishes a routine that can continue monthly throughout the year. The second provides children with an introductory problem-solving experience. The last two lessons in this section use children's first names to address a variety of arithmetic concepts and skills. Three of the four lessons use children's books as springboards for the learning.

Each of the next three sections focuses on one of the essential aspects of arithmetic: computation, problem solving, and number sense. It's important to keep in mind that these categories overlap. Therefore, while each lesson addresses the specific category of the section in which it appears, it also involves children with the other two categories. The lessons make use of children's books, manipulative materials, daily classroom routines, and contexts familiar to first graders. While there is no set sequence in which to teach these lessons, the lessons are ordered in each section from the least to the most challenging.

CHAPTER ONE
BUILDING THE CALENDAR

Overview

This lesson uses the housekeeping task of setting up the monthly calendar to provide students experience with reading numbers, ordering them, and examining numerical patterns on a calendar grid. The activity becomes a problem-solving situation as students try to place missing numbers on the calendar grid. The activity is also useful for informally assessing students' ability to read and sequence numbers and their ability to count on from numbers other than one.

Materials

▲ large one-month pocket calendar with removable numbers
▲ month names, each written on a strip about 3 inches by 8 inches
▲ full-year calendar

Time

▲ one class period each month

Teaching Directions

1. Establish a place on the bulletin board to post the monthly pocket calendar, a full-year calendar, and the months of the year in order.

2. To begin the activity at the beginning of each month, clear the numbers from the monthly calendar. Have students identify the name of the month, and place it at the top of the calendar grid. Then ask them to use the last day of the previous month to decide where to place the card with the number 1 on this month's calendar.

3. Select other number cards, one by one. For each, have students read it and then place it on the calendar in the correct place.

Teaching Notes

As do many other primary teachers, I now have a large calendar in my room that displays one month at a time. I have the kind of calendar that has clear pockets and cards for the numbers, but in the past I've used a laminated calendar with number cards that stick to it. I also post a one-year calendar so that the children can see how each month fits into the larger picture of the full year and to give them experiences using the calendar as we do in real life. The one-month calendar, however, helps us focus on the structure of a month and pay attention to numerical patterns.

Rather than post each month's calendar already put together, I plan a mathematics activity for the beginning of each month in which the students build the calendar and talk about its elements. I hang the calendar on a bulletin board within easy reach of the first graders. On the wall next to it, I post cards with the names of the months, arranged in order going down the wall so that students can see the order of the months and where the current month fits into the order.

Often, students think of the month when school starts as the first month of the year. This is understandable, as the first month of school begins a new cycle for the children, a cycle that's probably more important to them than is the calendar year. (As a teacher, I also often think of the year in terms of the school year.) However, children need to understand that the first month of school actually occurs after the middle of the calendar year, and the posted list of months helps develop understanding of this concept.

If the first day of the month falls on a school day, we build the calendar then; otherwise, we build it on the first school day after the month begins. We start by looking at the previous month on the one-year calendar.

The Lesson

▲▲

I gathered the children in front of the bulletin board that displayed two calendars. Posted there was a large one-month pocket calendar with removable numbers. Next to it were the months of the year, posted in order down the wall, each written on a separate strip. Also posted was a yearlong calendar.

"Who knows what month begins today?" I asked the students on the first day of September. In Texas, school starts in August, so the children had been in school for more than a week. I constructed the August calendar before the children arrived, and we had been using it daily to identify the day and the date. That way, by the time the first of September arrived, the children had had daily experience looking at the August calendar.

"September," the class responded.

"Can someone find the word *September* on the wall?" I continued.

Chanell stood up and pointed to the card posted on the wall with *September* written on it, just under the blank space where the month of August fit. I removed the August card from one-month pocket calendar and showed the class where it belonged. Then I asked Chanell to place the September card in the large pocket at the top of the calendar.

I next pointed to August 31 on the pocket calendar and asked, "On what day of the week did August end?"

Jacob raised his hand. "It was a Tuesday," he said. He moved his hand from the 31 up the column until he got to the word *Tuesday* at the top of the calendar.

"So, on what day does September start?" I asked.

"On Wednesday," Crystal answered.

Next, I quickly took all the numbers out of their pockets. I handed the number 1 to Crystal to place on the calendar. She started to put it into the Wednesday slot next to where the 31 had been at the bottom of the August calendar. Lori jumped up and said, "If you put it there, Crystal, the other numbers won't fit. You have to put it in the first row." Lori pointed to the pocket where the first of September should be, and Crystal slipped the number 1 into place.

Next, I pulled out the number 4 and called on Rick to find its place on the calendar. When he slipped it into a pocket, I asked, "How do you know it's supposed to go there?"

"I counted from the one," Rick responded.

"Come show us how you did this," I pushed. Rick came up, put his finger on the 1, and counted to the space where he had placed the 4. I then held up the card with the number 7 on it.

"Who would like to place this card where it belongs?" I asked. I called on Kiana and gave her the card. As Rick did, she put her finger on the 1, counted forward out loud to the seventh place, and put in the card. "It's Tuesday," she also offered. Since Kiana had clearly shown how she had decided where to place the number, I didn't question her further.

The next number I chose was 13. I knew this would pose more of a challenge for the students, but I felt it was accessible for most students to place by using the same strategy as Rick and Kiana had, counting from the number 1. I also chose 13 as a way to assess who was confident placing it, who seemed tentative, and who was unwilling.

"Who can read this number?" I asked. Several children raised their hands, and I made a mental note of those who didn't.

"Let's say the number together quietly," I then said. I heard a chorus of "thirteens."

I asked, "Who would like to come up and place the thirteen card where it belongs on the September calendar?" I called on Ignacio.

When Ignacio came up to the calendar, he first put his finger on the 7 and then moved it along, counting to himself. I didn't interrupt him because I've learned that when I do so, children often lose confidence in what they're doing. Instead, I decided to ask him to explain after he placed the number, as I had done with Rick. I knew that not all children would be comfortable counting on from the 7 to place the number 13, and I hoped that Ignacio's explanation would give others access to this idea.

Ignacio placed the number correctly. When I asked him to explain what he did, however, he resorted to counting from the number 1.

I said, "I noticed that when you first placed the number, you put your finger on the number seven, not on the number one. Can you tell us what you were doing then?" Ignacio then showed us what he had first done, putting his finger on the 7 and counting aloud up to 13.

I commented, "It seems to be quicker if you count on from the seven instead of going back to the one. That's a good strategy to use." I didn't say any more about that.

The next number I held up was 20. As I had done with the 13, I asked who could read the number and then had children say it aloud in unison. I called on Melony to place it.

Melony first started to count from the 13 but then got confused. "Can I start over?" she asked. I nodded.

Melony then started to count from the 1. She seemed encouraged by landing correctly on the 4 and the 7, but she got confused making the transition from the end of the row with the 7 in it to the next row and lost count. She looked at me for help.

"How about putting your finger on the seven and starting from there?" I suggested gently.

Melony did so, made the transition to the next line correctly, but then got confused after the 13. I helped her, putting my finger with hers on the 13 and counting aloud with her until we reached the 20. She inserted the number card and seemed relieved to sit down.

I continued the activity in the same way, holding up a number card, asking the students to read the number, and having a volunteer place it on the calendar. At the beginning of the school year, I take the time to have students place every number. We talk about each number as it goes up. The numbers I choose at this time of year are close enough together to be fairly easy while still presenting a challenge. I choose the numbers from the stack at random, but I think carefully about which number I want each child to place. Later in the year, I sometimes just assign the task of building the calendar to a few children who are still having trouble with number order.

Throughout the activity, I observed which students could place their numbers with ease and which had difficulty. I noticed which students went back to the 1 to count and which started with the largest number before the number being placed. I observed the students' ease with the return sweep to the next line when they were counting. All of these observations informed my decisions about mathematical experiences and discussions I wanted to have with my students in the future.

EXTENSIONS

As the year goes on, I begin each month by placing the number 1 first, but then I change the activity in subtle ways. For example, I begin the next few months by modeling how to place a number to review the activity for the class. One way I do this is by asking who has a birthday that month, and we place those numbers first. Also, sometimes I point to blank spots on the calendar and ask students to identify the missing numbers.

Later in the year, I focus on the patterns on the calendar, for example, that the numbers increase by one going a space to the right and decrease by one going a space to the left. While these patterns are obvious to adults, they aren't to all children. Also, I point out that a number underneath another is seven more, and I relate that to the seven days of the week. We practice adding seven to some numbers and check to be sure that the total represents the correct date for the space below.

I continue to give the class practice reading the numbers, and I talk about the different numbers of days in the months. Sometimes I remove all of the cards with the months on them and have the children use the yearlong calendar to help me replace them in order. Throughout the year, the monthly task of setting up the calendar becomes an opportunity for counting, sequencing numbers, and exploring patterns.

Questions and Discussion

▲▲

▲ *Many primary teachers I know add a day to the calendar each day. Why do you build the whole month's calendar at once?*

The only place you'll ever see a calendar built one day at a time is in a primary classroom. I used to have my students add a calendar piece each day as part of our morning routine, but a colleague helped me see that this isn't an accurate model of this timekeeping tool. In the real world, we use calendars to help us plan, keep track of appointments, and measure time. I want to model those uses for my students, and therefore, it's important that they can see the whole month at once.

I also think it's important to have a complete one-year calendar posted nearby, so that we can both plan ahead and think about events that have already occurred. It's important for children to know the order of the days of the week and the months of the year. But more important, they need to understand the structure of the calendar and how to use it to answer questions such as how many days there are until an expected school event or how long ago we celebrated a holiday.

▲ *Why did you ask children each time to explain how they determined where to place the calendar numbers?*

I've learned to ask children to explain their reasoning even when, as Rick did, they respond correctly. That way, children don't automatically think they are wrong if I raise a question about what they did. Also, when a child explains, the others have the benefit of hearing how one of their classmates reasoned. And if the child made an error, he or she has a chance to catch his or her own mistake.

▲ *It seems that the calendar activity is good for teaching the children how to count on from numbers other than one. Do you have more suggestions about how to do this?*

Learning to count on from numbers other than one is a useful skill for first graders to learn, but children first must have confidence in the counting sequence and in what they understand about how numbers work. I support their learning to count on by bringing this strategy to their attention as often as possible. One benefit of the calendar experience is that it will be repeated each month, thus giving me several opportunities to bring children's attention to counting on. I offer encouragement each month, but I know that children learn at different rates and won't necessarily learn from one particular experience.

CHAPTER TWO
GOOD NIGHT, GORILLA

Overview

The children's book *Good Night, Gorilla,* by Peggy Rathmann, is the springboard for this lesson, involving students in a beginning numerical problem-solving experience for which multiple approaches are suitable. After hearing the story and establishing the cast of seven animals and two people, the children solve the problem of how many feet there are altogether. They use words, pictures, and numbers to represent the problem and their solutions, and later compare answers and explain their thinking during a class discussion.

Materials

▲ *Good Night, Gorilla,* by Peggy Rathmann (New York: Putnam, 1994), big book version if possible
▲ objects for counting, such as cubes, tiles, or other materials, about 35 per student

Time

▲ one class period

Teaching Directions

1. Show the children the cover of *Good Night, Gorilla* and ask them to make predictions about the story. Then read the book aloud and discuss the setting, the characters, and the action in the story.

2. Pose this question: "When all the characters are together in the zookeeper's house, how many feet are in the room?"

3. Ask the students to identify all of the characters in the story. Make a sketch of each on the board, being sure to show his or her feet.

4. Give students directions for solving the problem. Tell them that they are to figure out how many feet were in the bedroom when all of the characters were there. Also, they should title their papers *Good Night, Gorilla* and then use words, pictures, and numbers to solve the problem and explain their thinking.

5. After children have worked on the problem, initiate a class discussion focusing on their strategies and recording methods. Also have students compare solutions.

Teaching Notes

Good Night, Gorilla, by Peggy Rathmann, a nearly wordless book, tells the simple, funny story of a tired zookeeper making his rounds at the zoo, checking the animals in their cages and saying good night. After he says good night to the first animal, the gorilla, he doesn't notice that the gorilla has picked his pocket and now has his keys. The gorilla, accompanied by a mouse carrying a banana, follows the zookeeper on his rounds. As the zookeeper moves on past the elephant's cage, the gorilla unlocks the cage and lets the elephant out. The gorilla, the mouse, and the elephant walk on together behind the zookeeper to the lion's cage, which the gorilla also unlocks. Soon a parade of animals forms as the gorilla frees the rest of the animals. Sleepily, the zookeeper trudges home, followed by the gorilla and the small mouse, the elephant, the lion, the hyena, the giraffe, and the armadillo. They follow him into his house and into his bedroom, where they all settle down to go to sleep. The zookeeper's wife is already tucked in with her eyes closed and doesn't notice at first that the room is filled with animals. As she pulls the cord on her night-light, she says to her husband, "Good night, dear." On the next spread, six speech bubbles of various sizes all contain the words "Good night." The completely black spread that follows shows one pair of very surprised eyes. The light goes back on as the zookeeper's wife looks around to discover her room full of uninvited guests. She lines them up, takes them back to the zoo, and then heads home. However, the gorilla looks out at us from the pages of the book with his finger to his lips as he follows the zookeeper's wife back home. Again she says, "Good night, dear," as she turns off the light. This time even she is too tired to notice the small "good nights" from the gorilla and the mouse as they snuggle into the zookeeper's bed and fall asleep.

At the beginning of first grade, I find it useful to work through a problem together with my class to help the children learn what I expect of them when they solve problems. I use *Good Night, Gorilla* to present a problem situation for several reasons. The context of the story makes the problem clear to the children, the mathematics is simple enough so that the problem is accessible to all of the students, and the problem engages children in identifying the pertinent information to be used in solving a problem. Also, the lesson gives children experience representing numerical information, either concretely, pictorially, or symbolically. Coming to know that quantities can be represented by pictures, manipulatives, or symbols is an important step for young children.

Solving a problem together as a class allows me to model problem-solving strategies as well as discover which strategies my students bring to a problem situation. Often children have good ideas about how to begin solving a problem, but they may not have confidence in their strategies. When I work with the class, I can encourage students and give status to their approaches.

This problem lends itself to multiple strategies, which makes it a good one for the beginning of the year because it gives students the message that there are many ways to arrive at a solution for most problems. Students also use counting skills to solve this problem.

The Lesson

▲▲

I observed a colleague, Mary Karnick, teach this lesson. Before she read *Good Night, Gorilla* to her first-grade class, she opened the big book and set it on an easel so that children could see the entire cover, front and back.

"What can you tell about this book just by looking at the cover?" she asked.

Tom answered first. "It's about animals," he said.

"There's a monkey in it," Beth added.

"It's like a monkey," Mary said, "but it's really a gorilla, maybe a baby gorilla."

"I think it's night-time," Justice said.

"How can you tell?" Mary asked.

"Look at the sky," Justice said, pointing from his place on the rug. "And the man has a flashlight."

Electra raised her hand. "I think the gorilla is saying, 'Shhh!' because his finger is like this." Electra demonstrated by putting her finger to her lips and making a "shhh" sound.

"He's got a key, too," Asia added. "And the man looks like he's sneaking somewhere."

"Who do you think the man might be?" Mary asked.

"A policeman?" Carter suggested.

"One of those guys who stands outside stores and makes sure nobody robs it," Donishia suggested.

"I think you mean a security guard, but that's not who he is. He's a zookeeper, and these are some of the animals from the zoo," Mary explained.

Mary knew that it was important to take the time to identify the characters and the setting for the story before she began to read, since many of the students in her class spoke English as a second language or had limited English experiences in their own neighborhoods. "I wanted to be sure that we had a common vocabulary to use when we talked about the characters and the story," Mary later told me.

The class talked about each character in the cover picture. The giraffe, the armadillo, and the hyena were unfamiliar to some students. They speculated about what the zookeeper and the animals could be doing out at night. Then Mary opened the book, and together, the class began to tell the story. Mary pointed out the speech bubble on the first page and read the words, "Good night, Gorilla." After that, the children chimed in with her for all the "good nights" and giggled as the gorilla set each animal free.

"This book provides a great opportunity for oral language development for young children," Mary later commented. "The story line is simple and the characters are amusing. Children notice the subtle humor in the pictures—the Babar doll in the elephant's cage, the stuffed hyena in the hyena's cage, and the keys that match the colors of the cages. There's more to the story than meets the eye at first glance. Children are drawn in to the story and this helps them be involved in the mathematics that comes later."

When she finished reading the story, Mary turned to the page showing all the characters in the bedroom while the zookeeper's wife turns on the light. Mary asked, "How many feet are in the bedroom right now?"

"I can't see all the feet. Look, you can only see the giraffe's head," Ricardo said.

"And the gorilla is under the covers," Asia said.

"All the animals are hiding their feet!" Donishia complained.

Mary then closed the book, which prompted a cry of, "Now we can't see any of the animals!"

After quieting the children, Mary posed a question to help them think about the problem. "How could we go about figuring out this problem?"

"Who was in the bedroom?" Blessing asked.

Mary responded, "That's right, we do need to think about who was in the bedroom. Let's make a list of the characters." As students called out the names of the animals, Mary drew a rough sketch of each, being sure to include its legs. She wrote the animal's name next to each of her drawings. When she had drawn the seven animals, the class was out of suggestions for her.

"Do we have all of the characters?" Mary asked.

"Oh!" Donishia exclaimed. "We forgot the zookeeper and Mrs. Zookeeper!"

Mary drew and labeled a sketch for each. When the students checked and agreed that they had a picture of each character, Mary gave the students directions for what they were to do next. "When you go back to your seats, you'll try to figure out how many feet were in the bedroom when all of the characters were there. On your way back to your desk, pick up a piece of paper here on this table. At the top of the paper, you need to copy the title *Good Night,*

Gorilla. Then use words, pictures, and numbers to solve the problem and explain your thinking."

"What if we can't draw animals?" Chase asked.

Blessing answered. "We could use tally marks like we do when we do lunch count in the morning."

"Maybe we could just draw the feet," Joey suggested.

Mary commented, "You can draw just the feet if you want to, or you can use something to represent the feet, like Blessing's idea about tally marks." There were no other questions, so Mary instructed the students to each take a piece of paper and return to their seats. Mary had put out unlined paper for this first problem-solving experience of the year.

As she walked around the room, Mary watched for children with questions. She stamped each child's paper with a date stamp for future reference and checked to see if any students needed extra help.

Asia's paper was blank after about five minutes, so Mary asked her, "What could you do to get started? Do you remember who the characters are?"

Asia thought for a moment and then said, "Mr. Zookeeper. He has two feet."

"What can you write for Mr. Zookeeper?" Mary asked.

Asia wrote *MZ* and drew two straight lines under the letters.

"That's a great start," Mary said. "You can use that method for all the characters." (See Figure 2–1.)

Donishia had many tally marks on her paper. Mary asked her, "Can you explain what you're counting here?"

Donishia pointed to the first tally marks. "See right here? These are the gorilla's feet." She moved her finger on. "And these are the elephant's feet."

Mary said, "I can tell that you know what these marks mean, but it's hard for me

▲▲▲▲▲▲Figure 2–2 *Donishia made tally marks to represent the feet, but she needed a system to keep each animal separate from the others. Mary's questioning led her to draw boxes around each animal's feet. She counted a total of 20 feet.*

▲▲▲▲▲▲Figure 2–1 *After Mary helped Asia get started labeling her marks, Asia was able to keep up with the characters so that she was sure she was counting all of their feet.*

to know without you telling me. What could you do that would help me know what all these lines represent when I look at your work after school?" Donishia thought for a minute and then drew a box around the first four tally marks.

Mary asked, "Whose feet are those?" Donishia wrote the letter *G* next to the box she had just drawn. Donishia then continued grouping and labeling the tally marks she had made. (See Figure 2–2.)

When Mary noticed that most students were finished or getting fidgety, she called the class to the circle. She already had in mind the strategies of several students that she wanted to share with the class. But first she asked for volunteers to share their work. Mary didn't focus on the answers they got but instead pointed out the similarities and differences among their strategies. After Donishia showed her work with the tally marks now in groups to indicate the legs belonging to each animal, Mary asked Asia to share her strategy to offer another alternative. Then Monica showed her recording, which was completely different. She had drawn a little tentlike mark for each foot and labeled the marks with numbers as well as letters. (See Figure 2–3.)

Mary later told me, "Not all children are eager to share their work. My ESL [English as a Second Language] children often have a lot to share on paper but don't have the language to express themselves. I try to get

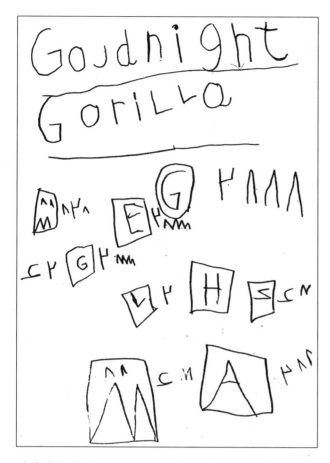

▲▲▲▲▲Figure 2–3 *Monica's writing still had many reversals, as is common at the beginning of first grade. But her work showed organization, as she used marks to represent the feet, then labeled them with letters as well as numbers. She counted 24 feet.*

them to stand and hold their papers up while I lead them through an explanation by asking questions about what they put on their papers. This lets them know that I value their thinking and not just their ability to describe it. This works for shy children as well, and I generally ask them in private if I can share their work with the class. The validation they get from hearing me talk about their strategies helps them feel more comfortable coming forward on their own next time."

Mary was not surprised to see that some of the children had made records of all the feet in the bedroom but didn't have totals to

share. "This was the first problem of this kind we did this year, and there were many things for them to focus on at once. For some of them, just making a representation of the characters was a big job," she told me.

The students in Mary's class were puzzled by the fact that everyone didn't get the same answer when counting the feet in the bedroom. She asked them, "Why do you think you didn't all get the same answer?"

Monica raised her hand. "Somebody might have counted wrong."

Electra suggested, "Maybe they drew too many feet."

"Or maybe they forgot an animal," Justice said.

Blessing and Beth had been holding their papers close together and whispering about their answers. Blessing spoke. "I think the mouse has four feet, but Beth only drew two." The class talked for a minute about the mouse and how the difference in opinion about feet would affect the answer.

"Not all my students were able to solve this problem successfully, but all were able to make a start," Mary told me. "My goal for the lesson was to introduce the children to a problem with many possible strategies and see what they could do with it. They had an opportunity to think about the problem on their own, talk about it with others, and record their thinking. They also had a chance to hear the strategies of their classmates. I think this is a good problem at the beginning of the year."

It's also a good problem to give again later in the year. Comparing the two sets of papers is a way to assess children's progress. Later in the year, you might also focus on the different ways children arrived at the answer as well as how they represented the problem. Figure 2–4 shows how another student solved this problem.

▲▲▲▲▲▲Figure 2–4 *Although it looks as if Joey counted groups of five feet, he actually drew lines to represent four feet for each animal. He made the slash marks as he counted them, to keep up with which ones he had counted already.*

Questions and Discussion

▲▲

▲ *Mary put out unlined paper for the children to use. Why is that important?*

In response to this question, Mary commented, "I used to use lined paper mostly, but I found that children are less constrained when I use unlined paper. With lined paper, they felt they needed to write carefully on the lines and thought they couldn't use pictures. Some were so worried about being neat that they forgot to focus on the math. Unlined paper allows them to write, draw, and organize their papers the way they want to."

▲ *How did Mary help her children learn to use tally marks?*

Using tally marks to represent objects is a useful tool for children and is best learned from firsthand experiences. In her classroom, Mary used tally marks to keep track of the number of children who were buying lunch and milk each day. She had modeled many times for the children how to group tally marks into fives, and while some children caught on more quickly than others, after a while, they all were comfortable using this system.

▲ *Even though the thrust of the lesson was for children to see different ways to represent a problem situation, isn't the answer also important?*

Answers are important, and it's fine to focus on the children's solutions as well as their representations, especially if you use the problems again later in the year. When doing so, however, be sure to focus on the ways children reached their answers and push children to explain how they reasoned. For example, many children at the beginning of the year will solve the problem by representing the legs and then counting them. Most will count the legs by ones, but counting by twos is another way to check. Later in the year, children might choose to add the seven fours and the two twos. It's valuable for children to see that there are multiple approaches to solving problems, and this is a good example to illustrate that.

CHAPTER THREE
INVESTIGATING NAMES

Overview

In this three-day math lesson, children have experience with sorting, counting, comparing, and estimating while becoming familiar with one another's names. On the first day, the children are involved in sorting their names by examining characteristics of their names and deciding how these characteristics are similar to and different from those of their classmates. In the second day's activity, students write the letters in their names on sticky dots, put each dot on an interlocking cube, and snap together the cubes to build a name train. The concepts of greater than, less than, and equal are discussed as students compare their cube trains. On the third day, the students work together to find the total number of letters in their first names. They snap all of their name cubes together; estimate the total number; count the cubes by ones, fives, and tens; and finally use standard notation to record the total. This lesson also makes use of the children's book *Chrysanthemum*.

Materials

- ▲ *Chrysanthemum*, by Kevin Henkes (New York: Greenwillow Books, 1991)
- ▲ construction paper cut into 3-by-18-inch strips, each folded into twelve equal parts (fold paper in thirds, then in half, then in half again), 1 per student

▲ $\frac{3}{4}$-inch sticky dots, any color, enough so each student has a dot for each letter in his or her name

▲ interlocking cubes (Snap, Unifix, or Multilink), enough so each student has a cube for each letter in his or her name

▲ one-inch squares, 1 sheet per student (see Blackline Masters)

Time

▲ three class periods

Teaching Directions

DAY 1

1. Show children the cover of *Chrysanthemum* and ask them to predict what it's about. Then read the book to the class.

2. Have children discuss their names. Make a chart of "Names We Like to Be Called" and "Names We Don't Like to Be Called."

3. Distribute 3-by-18-inch strips of construction paper, folded into twelve parts, and ask each child to write his or her name on a strip, putting one letter in each space. Model by writing your name on a strip.

4. Gather the students in a circle and direct them to get in groups with others whose names are like theirs in some way. Ask each group to describe how its members' names are alike.

5. Ask students to sort themselves again using different criteria. This time, instead of having the children report how their names are alike, have them try to figure out the common attribute for each group.

DAY 2

1. Reread *Chrysanthemum*.

2. Instruct students to write the letters of their names on sticky dots, place the dots on interlocking cubes, and snap the cubes together to build name trains.

3. Show the children a sheet of one-inch squares. Hold it sideways so that there are seven rows with nine squares in each. Show the children how to locate the middle row.

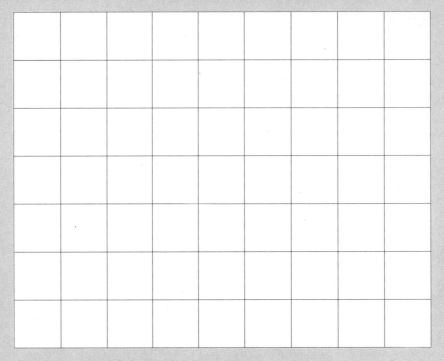

4. Distribute to each child a sheet of the one-inch squares and instruct them to write their names in the middle row, one letter per square. (Prepare extra paper strips if needed for longer names.) Prepare a paper with your name written in the correct row.

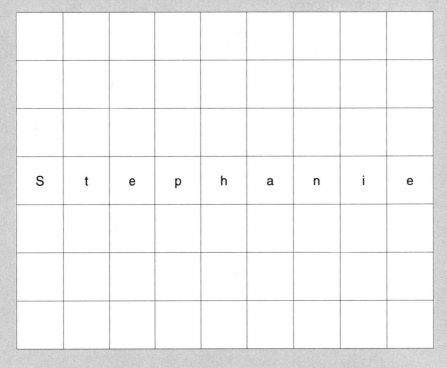

5. Ask a child to join you at the front of the room with his or her name train and grid paper. Compare your name trains. (Be sure not to choose a child with the same length name as yours.) Talk about whose name is longer and whose is shorter.

6. Tell the children that they are to write on their grid papers three shorter names in the rows above theirs and three longer names in the rows below. Model this by writing the name of the volunteer child in the correct place on your grid paper. Students with very short or very long names may not be able to complete their sheets. Ask them to think of names of people in stories that they could use to fill in the rows.

7. Post the children's papers and encourage the class to examine them.

DAY 3

1. Ask the students to sit in a circle and put their name trains on the floor in front of them.

2. Ask the children to estimate the total number of letters in all of the names in the class. Accept all of their ideas.

3. Ask students to group themselves according to the number of letters in their names. Have groups get in order. Talk with the children about what they notice about the groups. Ask if anyone would like to change his or her estimate about the total number of letters in the names.

4. Have the children snap all of their name trains together. Count the cubes by ones. Then have them break the cubes into trains of five and count by fives. Finally, have them snap the cubes back together, break them into trains of ten, and count by tens.

5. Bundle together ten tens to make one hundred. Record on the board the number of hundreds, tens, and extras, and relate this to the standard notation for the total number.

6. For a final activity, have the children reassemble their name trains. You might make this an activity for a center, putting all of the cubes from the children's name trains in a bin or a basket and having children fish for the letters they need. Tell them that it's OK to use someone's else letter as long as they spell their names correctly. Then save their name trains for another activity (see Chapter 4, "More Investigating Names").

Teaching Notes

Chrysanthemum, by Kevin Henkes, is a sweet story about a baby girl mouse whose parents think she is absolutely perfect and so give her a name that is absolutely perfect: Chrysanthemum. Chrysanthemum loves her name until she starts school. There she is teased by other students who say that her name is too long to fit on her name tag. Victoria remarks that Chrysanthemum's name has thirteen letters in it—exactly half as many as in the whole alphabet! Chrysanthemum begins to think her name is perfectly awful.

With much love and patience from her parents, and some help from a very special teacher named Delphinium, Chrysanthemum grows to appreciate her name once more.

When I start a new year with a new class, my first goal is to build a sense of community. To do this, I often use the theme of names to help students get to know one another, and I use *Chrysanthemum* as a springboard for this exploration. Reading this book aloud is one of the things I most look forward to at the beginning of each school year. No matter how many times I read this story, I am always touched by Chrysanthemum's initial joy as she begins school and her subsequent pain when she doesn't fit in. I find this book to be a great way to begin a discussion with young children about what makes each of them unique and how we can best appreciate the uniqueness of each child in the class.

The activities in this lesson involve students with sorting, counting, comparing, and estimating. Young children benefit from repeated experiences with these skills in different ways. From many experiences, they begin to understand that counting in different ways won't produce different results. Working with a context that relates to the children themselves makes this problem meaningful. They see that numbers can help them answer questions about themselves and their surroundings and that numbers are useful tools for solving problems in their world.

The Lesson

▲▲

DAY 1

I gathered the children to read *Chrysanthemum* aloud to the class. First I showed them the cover of the book. "The title of this story is *Chrysanthemum*," I said. "Can you say the title along with me?" The children tried pronouncing the word a few times.

"What do you think this story might be about?" I then asked.

"A mouse," Brittany said.

"A girl mouse," Ann added.

"That's a big flower," Jake said.

"It's bigger than the mouse," Andrew said.

I said, "This flower has the same name as the book. It's a chrysanthemum. Chrysanthemum is also the name of the little girl mouse, and this is a story about her."

I then read the book aloud. After I finished it, I led the students in a discussion about their names and what made them special. I asked them to think about all the names they were called, which ones they liked, and which ones they didn't like. We made a chart listing nicknames and pet names in two columns: "Names I Like to Be Called" and "Names I Don't Like to Be Called." We talked about the importance of always calling people by the names they prefer.

Next I asked the children to go back to their desks and I gave them each a 3-by-18-inch strip of construction paper. I always use light-colored construction paper, like yellow or pink, so that the children's writing will show up well, and I use the same color for the whole class to avoid conversations about who gets which color. Also, before the lesson begins, I fold each strip into twelve parts, folding it first in thirds, then in half, and finally in half again. This folding is difficult for small hands to do, so I do it myself ahead of time.

I said to the children, "Write your name on your strip, one letter to a space, so that someone could read your name from left to right. Use a dark crayon so that others will be able to read your names from a distance." I modeled this for them by writing my own name on a strip. I directed the children who were shaky about writing their names to copy them from their name tags, which were attached to their desks.

When all of the children had written their names, I had the students stand in a big circle, holding their strips in front of them so others could read their names. Sometimes I have to move desks and tables around a bit to have enough room for a large circle without furniture in the middle.

I said to the class, "Rearrange yourselves so that you are sitting next to children whose names are like yours in some way." I don't give examples of how they might sort themselves because I want them to create their own sorting rules. Too often I've found myself making up the rules for sorting: everyone with shoelaces goes here, everyone with buckles goes there. But some of the most important work in sorting is creating the categories and deciding what goes in each. At this point, Zaron came to me with a puzzled look on his face. "I'm the only Zaron. Nobody's name is the same as mine."

I responded, "Well, you are the only Zaron in this class. In fact, you're the only Zaron I've ever met! But other people in our class have names that are like yours in *some* way. Do you see a part of someone else's name that is the same as part of your name?"

Zaron looked around. He walked up to a couple of children and held his name strip next to theirs. Finally he turned to me,

beaming. "Adrian's name has an N at the end, just like mine!"

There is typically confusion at this point. Whenever children are confused, as Zaron was, I respond by assuring them that they don't have to have the same name as someone else in the class, but rather can find a name that is the same in only one way. Sometimes, after most of the class is sorted, a few students still can't see where they might fit. I ask them to stand by me for the time being and watch the others. "When you see a group where you fit, you can join it," I tell them.

Finally, when everyone had found a new place in the circle, I asked for the children's attention. "Let's find out how you sorted yourselves," I said. "We'll go around the circle, and when we get to your group, each of you will say your name and tell why you got in the group you're in. Let's start right here." I indicated the group standing next to me with Allen, Cynthia, Dejanique, and Brittany.

After each child said his or her name, Brittany announced, "Our names all have an A."

Next to them were Danny and Colby. They said, "Our names both end with a Y." Danny held his name strip above Colby's so that his Y was directly above Colby's.

"We both wrote our names with a blue crayon," Trevel explained for him and Andrew.

Jake and Juan stood together. Jake said, "We both have Js, but his doesn't sound like mine." Juan added, "And we both have four letters."

Victoria and Vladimir were together, and most of the class thought it was because their names started with V. But they announced, "We have long names. Dejanique could have been with us but she was already with the A group."

We went all around the room, with each group reporting its sorting rule. Then I said,

"Some of you might have heard another group's rule for sorting its names and thought your name would fit there as well. Now you'll have the opportunity to put yourself in a new group. Rearrange yourselves in groups with someone whose name is like yours in a new way. That means that even though my name is long, I couldn't be in a group with Victoria again if I was with her the first time. I would need to find a different way to think about my name."

Students began to move around the circle, talking to one another and looking carefully at their classmates' names. This sorting took less time than the first. Children seemed to have a better idea of what was expected and had some new ideas from sharing in the group. Everyone found a place in the circle without my help.

When everyone was settled, I explained how they would report. I said, "This time, instead of telling us how your names are alike, you're just going to say your names out loud. Then the rest of the class is going to try to guess how you sorted yourselves."

Victoria and Cortney said their names first. It was challenging for the class to figure out how their names were similar. Finally, the class gave up, and Victoria and Cortney triumphantly pointed out the word *or* in each of their names. We continued around the circle with each group saying its names and the rest of the class guessing the rule. Sorting categories included names that had the same number of letters, started with the same letter, rhymed, were written in the same color crayon, had the same small words inside, contained double letters, contained a particular vowel, ended with a particular letter, began with a particular vowel, were long, were short, and had the same letter chunks, like *ch* and *sh*.

DAY 2

I began class the next day by rereading *Chrysanthemum*. Children enjoy hearing favorite stories more than once and there is a benefit in rereading good stories to children. With each reading, they notice new things about the story, the characters, and the illustrations. Also, rereadings refresh their memories and allow us to focus on different aspects of the story.

Today I wanted to focus on the length of Chrysanthemum's name. After reading, I asked, "How many letters are in Chrysanthemum's name?"

Brittany remembered. "In the story, Victoria said Chrysanthemum had thirteen letters in her name," she said.

Sherrod spoke up. "That's a lot of letters! My name only has . . ." He stopped to count quickly on his fingers. "Seven letters."

I continued, "Some of you already know how many letters are in your name and some of you don't. On each table I've put a basket of interlocking cubes and some colored sticky dots. I want you each to write your name on the sticky dots, one letter per dot. Use a crayon so we'll all be able to read the letters. When you've done that, put the dots on the cubes, and then snap the cubes together to build your name."

The children were eager to begin. They wrote the letters of their names on stickers, peeled them off their backings, and placed them on the cubes. I watched as the children snapped the cubes together to form their names. I didn't worry if the stickers didn't fit exactly on the cube faces as long as they could be read.

I noticed that Jake snapped his cubes so that his name read from right to left. I pointed to his train of cubes as I said, "Jake, put your cube train underneath your name tag. Do they look the same?"

Jake looked puzzled for a minute as he realized that his cube train didn't match the name on his name tag. First, he picked up the cube train and turned it upside down.

When that didn't work, he flipped the train end to end. Now the letters were in the right place, but they were upside down. This was a difficult problem for Jake. (He didn't always get the letters in his name in the right order when he wrote his name.) I reached down and unsnapped the J from the train and placed it under the J on his name tag. Then Jake unsnapped the other cubes, placed them under the other letters on his name tag, and snapped them together again. While he was doing this, other children who had already finished were comparing the lengths of their name trains with one another. I noticed that they often held their cubes vertically even though their names couldn't be read that way.

I asked the children for their attention and said, "I see that many of you are comparing your name trains with others around you. You're going to do some more comparing, and you'll also be recording whether someone's name is longer or shorter than yours. But right now, put your name train under your name tag and check to be sure you haven't left out any letters." Doing this would also help them check the direction of their names.

Next I held up a piece of one-inch squares. I showed them the name train I had previously made with my name on it. In kindergarten classes, I sometimes build my name train as a demonstration before children build theirs, but in first grade I prefer to have them work through how to build their own.

I held the paper sideways and asked, "How many rows are there on this paper?" The class counted to seven as I pointed to each row.

"How could I find the row in the middle of the paper?" I asked.

Shelby raised her hand. "You could fold the paper in half," she suggested. I folded the paper and unfolded it. Shelby then said, "Where the fold is, that's the middle row." I held the paper so that my fingers were at the beginning and the end of the row with the fold in it. Children were nodding their heads and agreeing that Shelby's method had worked.

I attached the paper to the chalkboard with a magnet and held my cube train above it. Then I demonstrated how to transfer my name into the squares in the middle row of the paper. I used a marker to write my name so everyone could see it. My name has nine letters and filled the row completely, with no spaces left over.

I then said, "Now you'll each write your name in the middle row. Fold the paper first to find the middle row, and then put your first letter in the square all the way on the left." I distributed the paper. For students who needed a little more help, I made a mark in the first box to indicate where they should begin writing their names. Some were being helped by friends sitting around them. Sometimes, children need help transferring their names one letter at a time into the boxes,

S	t	e	p	h	a	n	i	e

particularly when I do this lesson at the beginning of the year.

After all of the children had written their names, I asked for their attention so I could explain the next part of the activity. I took my record sheet down from the board and called Ashlee to the front of the room. I asked her to bring her name train and I held it first on top of mine and then below mine, lining up the first letters of our names.

"Is Ashlee's name shorter than mine or longer than mine?" I asked. It was easy for the class to see that Ashlee's name was shorter. I held up my record sheet next to the cube trains and pointed to the rows above my name. I said, "Since Ashlee's name is shorter than mine, I'm going to write her name above mine on the record sheet." I did this while the class watched.

I continued, "If I find someone whose name is longer than mine, I'll write it below my name on the record sheet. Now you'll compare your name trains with others in the room and try to find three people with names shorter than yours and three with

names longer than yours. Record the shorter names above yours on the record sheet, and the longer names below yours."

The children were very excited about this project and started walking around the room to compare names. Dejanique came stomping up to me in a couple of minutes with a look of frustration on her face. "I can't find anyone whose name is longer than mine." She thought for a moment and then said, "Except maybe Chrysanthemum's."

"Why not use her name then, Dejanique?" I responded. "You can also use names from other stories, if you can think of some." Dejanique went off to copy Chrysanthemum's name onto her paper, but I stayed close because I knew she'd be back soon with another question.

Sure enough, she popped up beside me with her paper. "It won't fit! Chrysanthemum's name is too long," she said.

I pointed out a tote tray with a roll of tape and a bunch of extra strips of one-inch squares. "You might want to add some squares to that row so that Chrysanthemum's whole name will fit," I said. Dejanique walked off happily with a strip in her hand.

Kia had the opposite problem. She had a hard time finding someone with a name shorter than hers. "If you can think of a story character whose name is shorter than yours, you can use it," I said. But Kia was having fun finding names longer than hers, and her name was in great demand as one of the shortest in the room.

Trevel and Andrew came to me with their record sheets. Trevel said, "I don't know where to write Andrew's name."

I asked, "What happened when you compared your name to Andrew's?"

Andrew and Trevel answered together, "They're the same length!"

I asked, "What names are you supposed to put above your own name?"

Trevel pointed to the rows above his name and said, "When someone's name is shorter than mine, I put it there." Pointing to the part of his paper below his name, he added, "And if it's longer than mine, I write it here."

"So, is there a place for names that are the same length as yours?" I asked. Andrew shook his head. He and Trevel went off in different directions to find other people to compare name trains with.

As children compared their name lengths with those of their classmates, they were becoming familiar with one another's names in several ways. They had the opportunity to put names and faces together, as well as to learn to recognize these names in print. They practiced writing others' names, copying one letter into a square at a time. For some this was easy, but for others it was a challenge, even with the trains of cubes sitting right on their papers. Observing the children as they worked through this activity helped me learn about their counting ability, their understanding of one-to-one correspondence, their ability to transfer a name onto a grid, and their concepts of more and less.

When the children finished, I posted their papers and encouraged them to examine one another's work. (See Figures 3–1 through 3–3.)

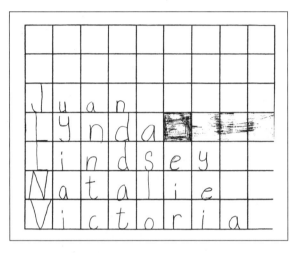

▲▲▲▲▲▲Figure 3–1 *Lynda was careful to use her best handwriting, but she found only one classmate whose name was shorter than hers.*

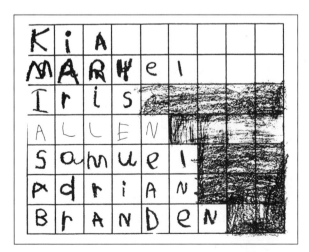

▲▲▲▲▲▲Figure 3–2 *Allen colored in the extra boxes, which highlighted the length of the names.*

▲▲▲▲▲Figure 3–3 *When Karina filled up all the spaces for names shorter than hers, she just made a dash and kept going.*

DAY 3

With our name record sheets posted around the room, we were ready to use the name trains in a different way today. I had the children sit in a circle on the floor with their name trains on the floor in front of them.

"Now we each know how many letters are in our own names," I said, "but I wonder how many letters we have in all our names put together." Several students recounted the cubes in their name trains. Others looked around the circle at the name trains on the floor.

Danny raised his hand. "I think there are about a hundred altogether," he said. Brittany nodded.

"Maybe two hundred," Taylor said.

"Maybe a thousand!" Juan offered.

"No, not a thousand, that's way too much," Shelby argued.

"What if we organized ourselves a bit? Do you think that would help us estimate?" I asked.

"I know!" Victoria exclaimed. "We could put all the kids with four letters together and all the kids with five letters together . . ." The words were barely out of her mouth when children began rearranging them-

selves. Shelby called the sixes together as the other groups began to form. Soon the children had sorted themselves into small groups scattered around the room. If Victoria hadn't made this suggestion, I would have done so.

"Here are the four-letter names," I said, indicating a rather large group. "And here are the nine-letter names." I pointed to the group standing next to the fours.

"What if we put these groups in order?" I said. "Where is the group with the fewest letters in their names?" Kia and Ann waved their hands.

"Come stand here next to the wall and the other groups can be next to you going across the room." With a little direction, the groups were soon standing in lines across the open part of the room.

"What do you notice about the groups now that you didn't notice before?" I asked.

Danny answered first. "It's easier to count how many are in each group now," he said.

"The sixes are the most," Jose commented.

"Do you agree, Juan?" I asked.

He answered, "Yeah, there are more sixes than any other number."

"This might give you a little more to go on when you make your estimates about how many letters are in all our names together. It's OK to change your estimate. When mathematicians get new information, they often change their estimates. Just tell someone else what you think and why."

I directed the class to sit down in a circle again so we could count the cubes. We started with the children who had three letters in their names. "Kia and Ann, snap your name trains together and hold up the new train." We counted together and got six cubes.

I pointed to the cube at the end of the train, with the letter N on it. "What does this cube represent?" I asked.

Samuel answered, "It's the N from Ann."

"Right," I said. "Every cube we count represents a letter in someone's name. So we're not just counting cubes; we're also counting the letters in our names."

I continued having the children snap their cubes onto the train that Kia and Ann had begun. We didn't count as we went along but just watched the cube train grow. When all of the students had snapped their cubes together, I asked, "How should we count?"

Lindsey crawled toward the cube train and said, "Just like, one, two, three . . ." The rest of the class joined in as Lindsey pointed to the cubes one at a time. This proved to be any inexact process because it was difficult for Lindsey to keep up with where her finger was on the long train of cubes. Together we counted 150 cubes, but I was pretty sure that Lindsey had missed a few cubes.

"What if we counted the cubes a different way? How else could we count them?" I asked.

"We could count by fives," Karina suggested.

"Or tens," Sherrod added.

"How would we do that?" I asked.

Branden answered, "We can just count five and snap them off." The children crowded in and started working at both ends of the cube train, snapping apart groups of five. In the end there were two cubes left in the middle of the train. We moved the two cubes off to the side and together we counted by fives to 150. Jaqueline picked up the two leftover cubes and we counted on to 152.

"I wonder how many there would be if we counted the cubes by tens," I said.

Danny responded immediately, "It would still be one hundred fifty-two." Danny was confident that no matter how we counted the cubes, the total would be the same, but other children in the class weren't so sure. I knew that just telling

them wouldn't be enough. Young children need many experiences counting and recounting in different ways for all of them to become confident that the number doesn't change when items are counted in a different way.

The children snapped all the cubes back together and then snapped off trains of ten. We counted fifteen trains of ten and had two cubes left over. I picked up ten trains of ten cubes and the children counted by tens with me, "Ten, twenty, thirty, forty, fifty, sixty, seventy, eighty, ninety, one hundred." I put a large rubber band around the ten trains, put them aside, and recorded on the board:

One hundred
100

Then we counted the remaining trains of ten: "Ten, twenty, thirty, forty, fifty."

"How many tens do we have here?" I asked.

"Five," they all answered. I put the five tens next to the bundle of one hundred cubes. I added to what I had already recorded:

One hundred	*fifty*
100	*50*

Finally, we counted from 150 to 152 as we moved the last two cubes next to the others. I added to the board:

One hundred	*fifty*	*two*
100	*50*	*2*

I then wrote a plus sign between each of the numbers, saying as I did so, "We have one hundred, and fifty, and two. One hundred and fifty and two is one hundred fifty-two." I recorded an equals sign and 152:

One hundred		*fifty*		*two*		
100	+	*50*	+	*2*	=	*152*

To end the lesson, I put all of the cubes into a bin and told the children, "I'd like you each to put your name train back together again so that I have a name train for each of you." I showed the children where I was putting the bin of cubes. "During activity time, you'll fish in the bin for the letters you need. Don't worry if the letter you pick out isn't one your wrote yourself; it's OK to use any cube that has the letter you need. When you have your name train made again, put it in this basket." I showed the children the basket. I gave this instruction because I planned to use the name trains for another math activity (see Chapter 4, "More Investigating Names"). Also, remaking their name trains provided the students reinforcement for identifying and sequencing the letters in their names.

Questions and Discussion

▲▲▲

▲ *What if my students can't come up with an idea for sorting their names? Should I give them a list of possibilities?*

I'm often a bit nervous when I give a direction as open-ended as this. However, experience tells me that children can do this, often coming up with sorting rules I would never have thought of. If your class seems to get stuck on one particular sorting rule, like the same number of letters, or the same first letter, just use your name to introduce a new idea. Think of a rule you'd like to use and find children whose names fit your rule. But then encourage them to think of and describe more of their own sorting groups.

▲ *At one point in the lesson, you pointed to a cube with the letter N on it and asked the children what it represented. Why did you do this?*

I think it's important to remind students repeatedly that the materials we use in math class often represent other things that would be harder to count or calculate. It's easy for young children to lose track of the original question and focus on the materials as if they were the thing being counted. I want children to know that manipulative materials help us model numbers in the real world and allow us to take them apart and put them together in new ways.

▲ *What kind of questions do you ask to extend the mathematics in this lesson?*

I think the most important thing to do when questioning first graders is to ask questions that require children to think and to express themselves with more than a one- or two-word answer. My goal when questioning is to find out what a child is thinking. Even incorrect answers give me insights into children's thought processes and help guide my instructional decisions.

CHAPTER FOUR
MORE INVESTIGATING NAMES

Overview

In this lesson, students count and compare quantities as they investigate which letters are used most and least frequently in their first names. For this investigation, the children use name trains made from interlocking cubes with stickers on which students write the letters of their first names. By taking apart their individual trains and sorting the cubes as a class by the letters in the alphabet, students figure out the total number of each letter in all the names in the class. The lesson blends literacy instruction with math as children discuss the letters in the alphabet and why some appear more frequently in their names. The lesson also makes use of the children's book *Martha Blah Blah.*

Materials

▲ *Martha Blah Blah,* by Susan Meddaugh (Boston: Houghton Mifflin Company, 1996)
▲ $\frac{3}{4}$-inch sticky dots, any color, enough so each student has a dot for each letter in his or her name
▲ interlocking cubes (Snap, Unifix, or Multilink), enough so each student has a cube for each letter in his or her name

Time

▲ two class periods

Teaching Directions

1. Show the children the cover of *Martha Blah Blah* and ask them to predict what the story is about. Then read the book to the class.

2. Ask: "Do you think a can of alphabet soup has all the letters in it? How many letters are there in the alphabet?" If children aren't sure about the number of letters in the alphabet, write the letters on the board and count them in at least two ways, by ones and then by twos, fives, or tens.

3. Next ask: "Do you think some letters of the alphabet are used more often than others, and some not so much?"

4. Ask children to stand if their first names begin with an A or if there is an A somewhere in them. Then suggest using their name trains to find out exactly how many As are in all of their first names together. Model with your name train, removing the A cube, if you have one. (If you aren't using this lesson as a follow-up to Chapter 3, "Investigating Names," have students construct name trains with interlocking cubes. To do so, they should each build a train with a cube for each letter in their first name, put a $\frac{3}{4}$-inch sticky dot on each cube, and then write a letter of their name on each sticker.)

5. When all of the children have contributed their A cubes, count them in at least two different ways, by ones and then by twos, fives, or tens. Then snap the A cubes into a train.

6. Ask: "Which letters do you think we have lots of in our names altogether? Do you think there are letters that we don't have in any of our names?" Continue through the alphabet, making a cube train for each letter.

7. Before class begins on the next day, arrange the letter trains to make a concrete graph. Place the trains vertically against a piece of poster board in alphabetical order and put sticky tack behind them so they remain standing. Leave a space for every letter that didn't appear in any name.

8. Gather the children around the graph and point to a cube. Ask: "What does this cube represent?" Repeat for a few more cubes to be sure that the children know that each cube represents a letter in someone's first name.

9. Then ask the children to examine the graph and report what they notice. Also pose questions for them to solve, drawing from the following suggestions:

▲ How can you use the R train to figure out how many cubes are in the S train? (Choose two adjacent trains and count the letters in one of them.)

▲ Which cube train has the most number of cubes? Which has the least?

▲ Which letters were used more often than others? (If you wish, talk about how every word must have a vowel, and perhaps that is why those letters are used so much. You may also wish to point out that the other letters are called consonants.)

▲ Do you think that the most common letter in your names is also the most common letter in all the words in the English language? (This is a complex question, and you should not look for a definitive answer. Rather, pose it to stimulate the children's thinking.)

Teaching Notes

Martha Blah Blah, by Susan Meddaugh, is the story of Martha, a dog who begins to talk after eating alphabet soup. Her vocabulary dwindles when the new owner of the soup company decides to save money and remove some of the letters from each can. The soup company's motto goes from "Every letter in every can" to "Letters in every can." The story tells how Martha discovers why she is having trouble communicating and how she inadvertently convinces the owner to replace the missing letters.

Not only is this a valuable math lesson, but it also fits nicely with the kind of letter and word activities I do at the beginning of the year. Whenever I can integrate two parts of my curriculum like this, I do so. But it's not so important to integrate two subjects that I would sacrifice an important mathematical topic just to fit in another theme we are studying in the classroom. The focus in math time must always be on mathematics. That may sound self-evident, but I find that as a primary teacher, sometimes I push to make everything fit a particular theme. I think it's important to resist this urge to make everything fit.

The mathematics in this lesson includes counting and comparing. The lesson also involves the children in interpreting data on a graph, in this case, a concrete graph made from trains of cubes. Just as it's possible at times to integrate math and literacy, it's also possible and valuable to integrate arithmetic learning with other topics in the math curriculum.

I typically use this lesson to continue the work begun with the name sorting, the comparing, and the counting that we did with the book *Chrysanthemum* (see Chapter 3) and use the children's name trains from that lesson. In this way, students have the opportunity to see that data can be manipulated in different ways to answer different questions. In the previous lesson, they used their name trains to determine the total number of letters in the students' first names. In this lesson, they reorganize the cubes from their name trains to determine which letters of the alphabet are used most frequently in their names.

Using cubes labeled for the letters in the students' first names, we build a graph to compare the frequency of each letter. Students compare the number of cubes for different letters, draw conclusions based on the collected data, and make statements expressing these conclusions. We talk about whether this sample is representative of all English words. Although first graders are not expected to answer tough questions like this with certainty, it's good to begin posing them. By considering complex questions, children come to see that there is more to think about than the activity of moving, snapping, and counting cubes.

The Lesson

▲▲

DAY 1

Before reading *Martha Blah Blah,* I showed the children the cover and asked them to think about what the story might be about. Lots of children raised their hands. I called on Adrian first. "Didn't we read another book about that dog?" he asked.

"Yeah, I remember," Sherrod said. "It's about Martha, the dog that eats the soup with letters. The letters go to her head instead of her stomach," he explained.

"That's right, Sherrod. The first book about Martha was called *Martha Speaks.* This book is by the same author and is a sequel to the first book. That means it has some of the same characters but the story will be new. What can you tell from the title?" I asked.

Victoria said, "You can't really tell what it's going to be about."

"But we know it's gonna be about Martha!" Vladimir added, smiling.

As I read this story to my first graders, it was important to share the illustrations. Not only is it difficult to read, "Goo oup o (Good soup today)," but some children didn't realize what was happening to Martha until they saw the spaces where the letters were left out.

When I finished reading the book, I asked, "Do you think a can of alphabet soup has all the letters in it?"

"How many letters are there?" Sarah asked.

"Twenty!" Danny replied.

"There are more than twenty," I said.

"Thirty?" Dejanique guessed.

"Fewer than thirty," I responded.

"Twenty-nine?" Adrian asked.

"Fewer," I responded.

The children kept guessing, reducing the previous guess by one each time until they got to twenty-six.

Rather than having the children take my word for the correct number, I decided to give them the opportunity to verify for themselves that there were indeed twenty-six letters in our alphabet. It's important to provide children the opportunity to check answers. Then they come to expect that answers are supposed to make sense.

I said to the class, "I'm going to write the letters of the alphabet on the board. See if you can say them as I write them." Even though the alphabet letters were posted above the chalkboard, I wanted to group

them in several ways to count them, so I wrote them on the board.

"Let's count and be sure we get to twenty-six," I said after I finished writing. I pointed to the letters one by one as we counted.

"But we should check to be sure that we're right," I then said. "I'll circle groups of fives and we'll count again." The class had been practicing counting by fives and most of the children were familiar with the sequence. I read the first five letters and drew a circle around them, then did the same for the next five and so on until all were circled except for the Z.

"Now let's count the fives," I said. I pointed to groups as we counted together, "Five, ten, fifteen, twenty, twenty-five, and one more makes twenty-six."

I then asked the class, "Do you think some letters are used a lot in words, and some not so often?"

Allen said, "I think there's a lot of As because there's Adrian, Allen, and Andrew."

I responded, "That's right; all of your names begin with A. Does anyone else have an A in his or her name?" Eight more children raised their hands.

"Mine doesn't start with A, but I've got an A in the middle," Branden said.

"So if we counted all the As in all our names, how many do you think there would be?" I asked.

Students called out their guesses. "A hundred!" "Twenty-five." "Thirty-five." Young children often make wild guesses without considering what would make sense. They often think of questions as riddles, not as problems that call for reasoning. Children need to be directed to think about reasonable estimates based on the information available to them.

To help the children think about information that could help them estimate, I said, "If your name begins with A, please stand." Six children stood and the class counted as I said their names, "Andrew, Adrian, Ann, Allen, Ashlee, April."

"That's six As so far," I then said. "Also stand up if you have an A anywhere in your name." Now fourteen children were standing.

"Wow! That's a lot of As!" Allen exclaimed.

I asked, "If we counted all these people, would we know how many As we have altogether in our names?"

Victoria raised her hand. "I don't think so because somebody might have an A at the beginning and an A in the middle."

"Yeah, like me," Adrian said.

I asked the students to sit down and then I called for the class's attention again. "I have another way for us to count all the As in our class." I brought out the basket of children's name trains that we had used for a previous exploration (see Chapter 3, "Investigating Names.") I showed them the train for my name, made from nine cubes snapped together, one for each letter in *Stephanie.* On each cube was a $\frac{3}{4}$ -inch sticker on which I had written one of the letters.

I pointed out the A in my name. Then I unsnapped my name train and put the A cube on the easel. I said, "Each of you will go back to your seat and look for As on your name train. If you find any, unsnap your train and bring the cubes with As on them to the front of the room. Then we'll put them together and figure out how many As there are in our names in all."

Zaron was reluctant to give up his A cube, but I reminded him that if he didn't, we couldn't count it. Learning to work as part of a group is still a challenge for first graders and gentle encouragement can help.

Before we snapped all the A cubes together, we counted them. With the stu-

dents gathered around me, I counted by ones, moving each cube as I counted, and got to twenty-four.

"Let's count in a different way to be sure," I said. "Who has an idea about how else we might count?"

Taylor said, "By fives." I let Taylor help me make *loose* groups of five with the cubes.

Then we counted, "Five, ten, fifteen, twenty, and four more makes twenty-four."

Next I asked the children, "Which other letters do you think we have lots of in our names altogether? Do you think there are letters that we don't have in any of our names?" Asking the children to make predictions often helps them invest in finding an answer, much as having them predict what might happen before I read a story helps build their interest in what I'm about to read.

"I know we have a Z!" Zaron announced.

"I think there's a lot of Ts," Tyler said.

"I've got one," Taylor said, adding evidence to Tyler's prediction.

"I have two Ns," Ann added.

"Me, too!" Danny exclaimed.

I quieted the children and said, "Let's use the cubes in our name trains to find out. We have a train of all the As. Now let's see about the Bs. If you have a B in your name, bring it up." As the children came up, I snapped their B cubes into a train. Although we didn't count the Bs, some children commented on the quantity, comparing it to the A cubes by noticing that it was shorter. Other students referred to the alphabet above the chalkboard to determine which letter cubes should be snapped together next.

I continued collecting cubes and making trains for the other letters in the alphabet. Some children were surprised to discover that there weren't any Fs or Gs. Others were surprised that some of the letters at the end of the alphabet were in our names even though they didn't know many "regular" words with those letters.

"There's only one Z," Zaron said proudly.

I gathered the trains onto a nearby table and left them there to use in the next day's lesson.

DAY 2

Before class the next day, I arranged the letter trains vertically to make a concrete graph. I placed the trains against a poster board in alphabetical order and put sticky tack behind them so they would remain standing. I left a space for every letter that wasn't in our names.

As the students came in, they stopped and admired the display. They talked to each other about which letter trains were the tallest and why certain letters were missing. Some found individual cubes and identified them as "my T" or "my S."

At the beginning of math time, I pointed out a cube with an E on it and asked, "What does this cube represent?" Many hands went up. Cortney was particularly excited, barely managing to stay in her seat. I called on her.

"That's my E!" she proclaimed proudly. "That's the E at the end of my name."

Then I pointed to a cube in the R trains. "What does this cube represent?" I asked. There was a moment of silence as no one claimed this cube.

"That's an R in somebody's name," Nitya finally answered. I wanted students to understand that, even if they didn't know whose name a cube came from, it still represented a letter in the first name of someone in our class.

"What can you tell me about our letter graph?" I asked.

"We had almost all the letters in the whole alphabet," Sarah said.

Danny added, "There are only two letters without cubes and . . ." Danny paused and looked at the ceiling as he thought. Then he added, "There are twenty-four letters with cubes."

Taylor raised his hand. "I think there are ten Rs," he said.

Shelby agreed with him. "That's what I counted, too, but there are less Ss."

I asked, "Can we use what we know about the Rs to figure out how many Ss there are?"

"That's easy," Victoria said. "You can just count down from ten." She pointed to the tenth cube in the R train and counted, "Ten, nine, eight, seven," as she moved her finger down the cubes in the R train. Then she slid her finger across to the seventh cube in the S train to show that it had seven cubes.

Sherrod raised his hand now. "The N tower and the R tower have the same number of cubes."

Adrian had been sitting quietly, looking intently at the graph, and I wasn't sure at the time whether he was hearing the other students' comments. But I knew that Adrian was a thoughtful boy so I decided to wait for his observations. Finally he raised his hand. When I called on him, he said, "I think some letters have bigger towers because almost everybody has them in their names. Like lots of us have an A or an E."

"You're right, Adrian; those are special letters. They are called vowels, and every word in English has at least one of them," I said. "Does anyone know another letter that is a vowel?"

Nobody raised a hand, so I recorded on the board as I said, "There are five vowels: A, E, I, O, and U. All words in English have one of those letters. But sometimes Y is also used as a vowel, like in the word *sky*. Think about your own name and see if you can find a vowel in it. Tell the person next to you what you find." Students talked quietly with each other, spelling their names out loud and exclaiming when they found a vowel. I called them back together.

"So, how many of you have a vowel in your name?" I asked. Every student raised a hand.

I then said, "The other letters are called consonants. We'll be learning more about vowels and consonants when we work with letters and words."

I then asked, "Do you think that the most common letter in your names is also the most common letter in all the words in the English language?" This is a complex question for which I wasn't looking for a definitive answer. Rather, I posed it to stimulate the children's thinking and give them something to ponder.

Nitya raised his hand. "I think there's probably a lot of As in all the words, because you see a lot of As when you read."

"My mom and I watch TV when we're eating dinner and *Wheel of Fortune* is on. People always get a lot of Ts and Ss. And everybody buys an E," Allen said. Other children nodded, indicating they had seen the program as well.

Zaron was somewhat philosophical about the matter. "I think all the letters are important, to make all the words."

Questions and Discussion

▲▲

▲ *If you and the children counted the twenty-four cubes carefully the first time, why was it important to count another way?*

I know that some children were convinced there were twenty-six cubes the first time we counted, but I didn't want to miss the opportunity to model counting in different ways and to practice the sequence for counting by five. First graders sometimes believe that if you count a different way the answer will change. They need many experiences with counting objects in many ways to understand that the number will always remain the same.

▲ *Had you planned to use this lesson to instruct the children about vowels and consonants?*

Teaching about vowels and consonants wasn't the goal of my lesson, but I think it was worth the detour. While we might separate instruction into time for math and time for reading, children don't make that distinction. For the children, learning is learning. I know that when I ask students what they notice about a graph, I'm opening the door for all kinds of observations—some mathematical, some not.

When I first began teaching this lesson, I prepared a list of questions about the letter graph. My questions were narrowly focused and usually had just one correct answer. But I've found that asking the more open question "What do you notice about this graph?" elicits a wider variety of observations and allows students to take a more active role in their own learning.

CHAPTER FIVE
RECORDING NUMBER SENTENCES

Overview

This lesson involves using the children's book *Ten Flashing Fireflies* to give students the opportunity to think about the various combinations of ten. After the children are familiar with the story and the action of moving fireflies into a jar, they represent the actions with addition and subtraction number sentences. The experience helps them see how addition and subtraction relate to each other.

Materials

▲ *Ten Flashing Fireflies,* by Philemon Sturges (New York: North-South Books, 1995)
▲ cubes, yellow or white if possible, 10 per student
▲ storyboards made from 9-by-12-inch black construction paper folded in half, with random dots dabbed on with white correction fluid on the left side and a glued-on cutout drawing of a jar large enough to fill up most of the space on the right side, 1 per student

▲ *Ten Flashing Fireflies* worksheets, 1 per student (see Blackline Masters)

Time

▲ two class periods

Teaching Directions

1. Show the children the cover of *Ten Flashing Fireflies* and ask them to predict what the book is about. Then read it to the class.

2. Read the book again, this time pausing before you turn each page so the children can predict the number of fireflies in the jar.

3. During the same lesson, or in a day or so, distribute to each child ten yellow or white cubes to represent fireflies and a storyboard, as described on page 34. As you read the book again, have the children use the cubes to represent the action.

4. For another reading of the book, gather children on the rug and have some of them act out the story and the others record corresponding number sentences as you read. Model for the children how to record by choosing a child and having him or her record for the first page of the book.

5. For additional individual practice, give each child a worksheet on which he or she can record the number sentences as you read the book again.

Teaching Notes

Ten Flashing Fireflies is a counting book about two children catching fireflies in a jar on a summer night. As the number of fireflies in the jar increases, the number of fireflies in the night sky decreases. Every two-page spread shows the fireflies in the jar on the left page and the fireflies in the night sky on the right page. The ten fireflies in the story are always in full view, although they are moved one at a time from the sky to the jar and, ultimately, back to the sky.

You can also use this lesson structure with other counting books. Some of my favorites include *Benny's Pennies*, by Pat Brisson (New York: Doubleday, 1993), *12 Ways to Get to 11*, by Eve Merriam (New York: Simon & Schuster, 1993), and *Monster Math Picnic*, by Grace Maccarone (New York: Scholastic, 1998).

The Lesson

▲▲

I showed the children the cover of *Ten Flashing Fireflies* and asked them to predict what the book was about.

Emily spoke first. "It's so dark! What is that on the cover?" I held the book out and walked around so that each child could see it close up. As I walked I heard "Ooh, what's that in the girl's hand?" and "There's someone else behind her."

Justin said, "I know what those are. We saw them at my Grandma's last summer, out in the country. They're lightning bugs!"

Several children looked puzzled, so I explained, "It is a kind of bug she has in her hands, and sometimes they are called lightning bugs. They are also called fireflies."

"Do they light up?" Misty wanted to know.

"Does it hurt to hold them?" Kylie asked.

As the resident expert, Justin spoke up to field those questions. "The back end of them glows like a light bulb, but they don't hurt. We caught them and held them. Their feet tickle your hands like a doodlebug." Now everyone in the classroom was eager to hear the story.

I read the book to the class. The children enjoyed the rhyming pattern of the story, as well as the soft, gauzy illustrations. Because the story takes place at night, the illustrations are all dark, so I continued to walk around and show the pictures to the children up close. The brightest page in the book shows the two children with ten bright fireflies in their jar. On the next page, the light of the fireflies dims as the children watch in alarm.

"The fireflies are dying!" Misty cried dramatically.

I turned the page to show the children opening their jar and recounting the fireflies as they fly away. The class cheered.

I then reread the book, pausing to ask students to make predictions as I went along. For example, I read: "What do we see in the summer night? Eight twinkling fireflies blinking bright! Let's catch another one. Now there are . . ." I stopped reading to let the students figure out how many fireflies would be left in the sky and how many would be in the jar.

I then turned the page and read, "Three twinkling fireflies in our jar." Students quickly begin to notice the pattern that the number of fireflies in the sky decreased by one while the number of fireflies in the jar increased by one.

I then read the book a third time. (Some years, I haven't done this third reading on the same day but have waited a day or two to return to the book. The children are always eager to revisit it.) Before reading it again, I distributed the storyboards I had made from 9-by-12-inch black construction paper folded in half. On the left side, I had created a night sky effect by dabbing on random dots of white correction fluid; on the right side, I had glued a simple drawing of a jar that filled up most of the space.

I said to the children, "I'm going to read the book again, and this time I want you to act out what's happening in the story by moving fireflies on your storyboards. We'll use these cubes to represent the fireflies." I showed them the basket of yellow and white cubes I had.

"How many cubes do you think you will need to act out the whole story?" I asked.

Ann raised her hand. "I think we need maybe. . ." She paused and looked at her fingers. ". . . Ten."

"Why do you think ten, Ann?" I asked.

"I think twenty," Emily interrupted. "There are ten in the sky and ten in the jar."

"But the ten fireflies in the sky all get caught in the jar," Ann replied, defending her idea.

"Oh yeah," Emily conceded.

I gave ten cubes to each child. "Since the fireflies are all in the sky when the story begins, put your cubes on the left side of your storyboard," I said. I waited until all of the children had done this.

As I reread the story, I watched to be sure children were correctly moving cubes from the night sky side of their boards to the jar side. In the book, you have to turn the page to see the jar holding the fireflies after they're caught. But when using the storyboards students are able to see all ten cubes separated into two groups and, therefore, see how the ten fireflies move from one place to another. This allows them to have a constant image of various combinations of ten. The students were delighted at the end to move all the cubes back to the night sky side as they counted down from ten to one.

In a variation of this activity, my colleague Maggie Lopez used a large piece of black poster board to represent the night sky and pasted on it a large cutout drawing of a jar. She cut ten 3-inch circles to repre-

sent the fireflies, put a splotch of yellow paint on each circle to make it look like the fireflies in the book, and then laminated them. Maggie used sticky tack to stick the fireflies to the jar or the night sky. She initially used this large model to illustrate the action as she read the book. Later, children used it to manipulate the fireflies and retell the story on their own.

DAY 2

On another day, I again returned to the book. I gathered the children on the rug and asked them to bring their individual writing boards. When the children were settled, I said, "Today some of you will act out the story while others record what is happening. Then we'll do it again so that all of you will have a chance to record the number sentences."

I asked for volunteers and chose two students to be the children in the story and ten to be the fireflies. The rest of the children sat on the rug with their small writing boards.

I gathered all of the fireflies to one side. "When you're here, that means you're in the sky," I said. I pointed to the rug area on my other side. "And we'll pretend that this is the jar."

As I read the first page, the volunteer children caught one "firefly" and led her to the imaginary jar. "Who has an idea what to record for this first page?" I asked.

"I think it's ten take away one is nine," Christine offered. "But the nine is on the next page."

"Will you come up to the board and record that number sentence?" I asked. I wanted to be sure that all of the children had a correct model for representing the action numerically.

"What will you write first?" I asked Christine when she came to the board.

"The ten because there are ten flashing fireflies," she said and then wrote *10* on the board.

"Show us the symbol we use to mean that one of the fireflies has left the sky," I continued.

Christine recorded a minus sign. I explained, "Christine wrote a minus sign, which means 'take away.' It tells that something has been removed from the group of fireflies. I can read what Christine wrote so far as 'Ten minus.'" Most of the students already knew this, since we had talked about the symbolism for subtraction in previous classes. Also, many of the children had older brothers or sisters who had taught them or parents who had shown them. Still, I think there's value in reinforcing such information and being explicit about the connections between mathematical symbols and what they represent.

Christine continued, "It's ten minus one, because they caught one firefly in the jar." She recorded *= 9* to complete the number sentence.

"Who can explain the part of the number sentence that Christine just wrote?" I asked.

Roger answered, "That's because there are nine fireflies left," he said.

"That's right," I agreed. "If you start with ten and you take away one, what you have left equals nine." By this time all the students on the rug had recorded on their writing boards: *10 – 1 = 9*.

"Now we have to record what happened to the number of fireflies in the jar," I said. "Do the number of fireflies in the jar get larger or smaller?" I asked.

Sarah answered, "Larger, 'cause they put more in."

"How many fireflies were in the jar when the story started?" I asked.

"None," Andrew said.

"How do we write *none*?" I asked.

"Zero," several children answered.

"I know," Christine said, still at the board. She wrote: *0 + 1 = 1*.

"Who can explain what Christine wrote?" I asked.

Kevin said, "There was zero and then one went in, so now there's one."

I asked Christine to rewrite the addition sentence so that it was next to the subtraction sentence she had already written. Then I continued with the story, following the same procedure for each page. I made sure that Christine wrote each addition sentence next to the corresponding subtraction sentence so that children could make the connection between the two actions. When I had finished reading the book, the children had two long columns of number sentences on their individual boards. Some had run out of room and had just erased the top and continued writing there.

10 – 1 = 9	0 + 1 = 1
9 – 1 = 8	1 + 1 = 2
8 – 1 = 7	2 + 1 = 3
7 – 1 = 6	3 + 1 = 4
6 – 1 = 5	4 + 1 = 5
5 – 1 = 4	5 + 1 = 6
4 – 1 = 3	6 + 1 = 7
3 – 1 = 2	7 + 1 = 8
2 – 1 = 1	8 + 1 = 9
1 – 1 = 0	9 + 1 = 10

"What do you notice about these number sentences?" I asked.

"The numbers count down, like ten, nine, eight, seven," Jordan observed, pointing to the numbers at the far left.

Emily jumped up. "But on this side," she said, pointing to the sums in the addition sentences, "the numbers start with one and go up to ten."

"Every time the number on the minus side goes down, the number on the plus side goes up," Terezia said. Terezia often needs to restate something in order to grasp it completely herself.

I thanked Christine and asked her to erase what she had written. Then I repeated the activity, choosing new volunteers to be the children and the fireflies and having the rest again record. This way, all of the children had the chance to record the number sentences at least once.

For individual practice a week later, I gave the students worksheets ruled into two columns. At the top of the left column, I had drawn a night sky with a black marker, leaving a few white dots to represent stars. I had drawn a jar at the top of the right column. As I read from the book, the students listened and recorded the number sentences, as we had previously done on the board. (See Figure 5–1.) A few used storyboards with the cubes to help them.

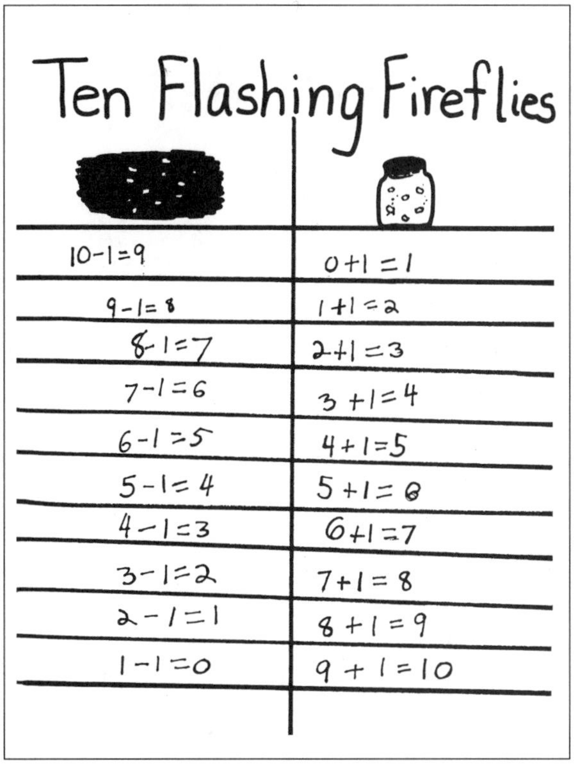

Ten Flashing Fireflies

$10-1=9$	$0+1=1$
$9-1=8$	$1+1=2$
$8-1=7$	$2+1=3$
$7-1=6$	$3+1=4$
$6-1=5$	$4+1=5$
$5-1=4$	$5+1=6$
$4-1=3$	$6+1=7$
$3-1=2$	$7+1=8$
$2-1=1$	$8+1=9$
$1-1=0$	$9+1=10$

▲▲▲▲▲▲Figure 5–1 *This recording is easier for students after they create the number sentences together on the board. It's still valuable practice for each individual child to do.*

Questions and Discussion

▲▲▲

▲ *Do you use all these activities every year when you read this book?*

How I use the book depends on the needs of that year's particular class. Sometimes I know that the children need to get up and move around, so the acting-out activity is appropriate. While I always have students work with the storyboards, some years I have children do so in pairs, and other years I choose to have them work with the manipulatives individually. Some years I've used the large display, as Maggie Lopez suggests, and other years it hasn't been necessary. Making these decisions is part of the art of teaching, and I decide based on what I know about the children and what I think will best help them grasp the mathematical ideas.

▲ *What is the benefit of having the children record on worksheets as compared with recording on individual writing boards?*

Using both is useful. The individual writing boards provide an alternative way for children to record. The combination provides the children some variety in how they do their written work. The worksheets, of course, result in a record of children's work that I can then check over to see who is having difficulty.

CHAPTER SIX
DEVELOPING OPERATIONS SENSE

Overview

The book *Splash!*, by Ann Jonas, provides an opportunity for children to experience addition and subtraction situations with a focus on the actions rather than on computing the answers. As they listen to the book, children decide whether the words they hear indicate addition or subtraction. They then use manipulatives to act out the movement of the characters in the book as they move into and out of a pond. The children also have to determine the total number of characters in the book as they move into the pond at the end of each page, which calls for counting or using mental computation.

Materials

▲ *Splash!*, by Ann Jonas (New York: Greenwillow Books, 1995)
▲ 6-by-9-inch blue construction paper, 1 sheet per student
▲ color tiles or other counters, about 15 per student
▲ cassette tape recorder and tape
▲ 12-by-18-inch white construction paper, 10 to 15 sheets
▲ 3-inch squares of construction paper, 2 per student

Time

▲ three class periods, spread throughout the year

Teaching Directions

1. Show the children the cover of *Splash!* and ask them to predict what the book is about. Then read it aloud to the class.

2. Distribute a 6-by-9-inch piece of blue construction paper to each student. Also make counters available for small groups of children to share, using only one color counter for each small group.

3. Read the first page of the story. Have children use the illustration to determine how many characters are in the pond. Ask them to put counters on their blue paper to represent the characters in the pond.

4. As you read the subsequent pages, be sure that the students add or remove counters to represent how many characters go into or come out of the pond. Then read the question at the bottom of the page: "How many are in my pond?" Have students use their counters to find the answer. Be sure all students agree before going on. Once students make an error, all of their subsequent answers will be incorrect.

5. At a later time, involve the class in creating a story based on *Splash!* First decide on a setting and characters, then on the actions. Record each action on a separate sheet of 12-by-18-inch drawing paper and later have children illustrate the pages. To follow up this experience, have children work in pairs and write individual stories.

6. Still later in the year, distribute two 3-inch squares of paper to each child. Ask them to write a plus sign on both sides of one square and a minus sign on both sides of the other. Reread the book, stopping after each page so they can each hold up one of the squares to indicate whether the action is addition or subtraction.

Teaching Notes

The book *Splash!*, by Ann Jonas, begins with the words of the little girl who is the main character. On each page, we can see both above and below the water of her backyard pond. The girl introduces one turtle, two catfish, three frogs, and four goldfish, and we can see that only the two catfish and the four goldfish are in the pond. We also see her sleeping dog and a bird on the birdhouse. Students are drawn into the story as they answer the girl's question, "How many are in my pond?" The story continues as the cat comes home and wakes the dog, which startles the turtle, who jumps into the pond. Again the girls asks, "How many are in my pond?" This time the class has to either stop and count the animals in the illustration or think about adding one to the total from the last page. The first four pages involve animals jumping into the pond, with a growing total. But from the fifth page on, the action gets more complicated as some animals get out of the pond while others jump in. The bright, bold illustrations and simple sentence structure invite children into the little girl's backyard.

Young children are exposed to the concepts of addition and subtraction even before they start school. Their lives are full of situations where quantities are combined or compared in some way, and instruction in school should connect these daily situations to the mathematical symbolism used to describe them. My goal is for children to become so familiar with the language of addition and subtraction situations that students recognize them immediately when they come up in story problems or in real life. One way to do that is to give the children practice with solving addition and subtraction problems before asking them to represent the problems symbolically.

The Lesson

▲▲

I gathered the children on the rug, showed them the cover of *Splash!*, and asked them what they thought the book was about.

Many children had ideas to share. "It looks like a lake," Mickey said. "Maybe somebody's going fishing."

"Something's gonna fall in the water and make a big splash!" Antoine said, using his arms to demonstrate the magnitude of the splash.

Rodney said, "There are going to be animals in the book."

Terezia explained, "There's going to be dogs, turtle, fish, birds, and frogs."

I then read the book aloud. The children were delighted by the pictures and the simple action of the characters. They loved the part where the dog and the cat fell into the pond, and they enjoyed keeping up with the total number of animals in the pond. Because of the relatively large pages, it was easy for the children sitting around me to count the animals in the pond to answer the question on each page: "How many are in my pond?"

After reading the book, I asked the students to return to their desks so that they could participate as I read the story. I distributed a piece of 6-by-9-inch blue construction paper to each child, and I placed a container of color tiles at each table. I had sorted the color tiles so that each container had only one color. I've found that when students have an assortment of colors, they sometimes try to assign particular colors to particular animals and then try to keep track of the colors as animals go into and out of the pond. Having children use just one color eliminates this possible confusion.

"As I read this book, you will use the color tiles to keep track of the action in the story," I told the children. I read the first page of the book aloud, stopping after I read the question

"How many are in my pond?" For this first page, we had to rely on the picture to determine how many were in the pond. But after that, children listened to the story to decide how to move their tiles. This can be challenging for some children for whom auditory processing is difficult, so I tried to read slowly enough for children to carry out one action before I read another. Also, as I read, I watched the way my students dealt with the question of how many were in the pond.

Near the middle of the book, I read, "The bird flies away." By this time, children had been putting in and taking out tiles for every sentence. I've learned that this sentence about the bird always catches a few, who remove a tile from the pond. But at least one child always says, "Wait a minute. The bird wasn't in the pond!" Then the other children laugh and replace the tile to their ponds.

Each time I've read this book to my class, the first thing they want to do at the end is to read it again. They seem to enjoy the interactive experience of answering the questions on each page. As I reread the story to this class, the students were more familiar with how to move the tiles into and out of their ponds, and they could focus more on the mathematics involved. Then I began to ask questions to further focus them on the mathematical action in the story.

"On this page, are we adding to the pond or subtracting?" I asked, pointing to the illustration on page 19.

"First we add," Melony said, "when the frog jumps in."

"What happened next, Antoine?" I continued.

"Then the turtle stays in, so we don't put any in or take any out," he replied.

"The little girl climbs out last," Lori said. "So that's subtracting, because you're taking away."

After reading the book to the whole class several times, I taped myself reading it, using a bell to signal when to turn the page. I placed this tape, along with construction paper and tiles, in the class listening center. I put the book there as well for children to refer to if they got stuck. At the center, the children could listen to the tape and keep up with the action with the color tiles, just as we did in the whole-class lesson, but they could also stop the tape and take as much time to answer the questions as they wanted. If they got confused, they could rewind the tape and listen again. This task was available to my students during math choice time, but other teachers in my building used it during literacy station work time.

LATER IN THE YEAR

I revisited the book later in the year. I reread it to refresh the children's memories about the format. Then I asked, "If we wanted to make up our own *Splash!* story, how could we change the setting to make the book different?"

Christopher had an idea. "I know, we could pretend it was a swimming pool. Kids get in and out all the time."

"Who has another idea? It doesn't have to involve water. What else could we use that things go into and out of often?" I asked.

"We could make animals go into and out of a barn," Chanell suggested.

"Or a zoo!" Alex added.

After talking some more, we decided to write a class version of *Splash!* using an African water hole as the setting, since we were studying African animals. The students decided on the animals that would be at the water hole and which of them would be in the water to begin with. As they dictated, I wrote the text on large pieces of construction paper. Because each page started with some animals in the water hole and some out, we had to keep close track of how each page followed the previous one. Unlike the times when we had read the book to find out how many were in the pond, when writing our book, we needed to keep track of which animals were where. In this situation, using different-colored cubes to represent the animals helped. After we wrote the text, pairs of children volunteered to illustrate each page. They enjoyed seeing the completed book and offered it to the class next door to read and solve. (See Figures 6–1 through 6–4.)

▲▲▲▲▲▲Figure 6–1   *The first step was to decide which animals were visiting the water hole.*

▲▲▲▲▲▲Figure 6–2 *I wrote the words on large paper after the class decided on the action for each page.*

▲▲▲▲▲▲Figure 6–3 *Keeping track of which animals were in the water and which were out was complicated.*

I then had students make up their own *Splash!* stories to tell each other. "You and your partner will decide on one setting for a *Splash!* story and take turns telling each other what happens each time. The other person will use tiles to show what is happening." This activity allowed more children to get directly involved in the storytelling. The class book can be a good way to introduce this activity, but it isn't absolutely necessary.

The lions went to their den and the other animals stayed at the water hole to rest and eat.

▲▲▲▲▲▲**Figure 6–4** *Every good story needs a good ending.*

STILL LATER IN THE YEAR

I often revisit the book later in the year to reinforce the language of addition and subtraction. Before the next lesson, I cut out 3-inch squares of construction paper, two per student. I distributed these and asked the students to each take out a dark-colored crayon.

I said, "Write a plus sign on each side of just one of the squares I gave you. Then, on both sides of the other square, write a minus sign." I waited until all of the children had done this.

"Now I'm going to read *Splash!* to you again," I said. I could tell by the applause and the cheering that the children were happy to revisit the book. "This time you aren't going to figure out how many are in the pond on each page. This time, listen to each sentence carefully and think about whether the action on the page is an addition action or a subtraction action. Who can describe what happens in addition?" I gave the class a few moments to think before calling on Kurt.

"When you add, you put things together," he said.

Lori said, "Adding makes the numbers get bigger."

"You're both right," I responded. "When we are adding things like people and animals into the pond, the total number will get bigger. How will you know when to subtract in the story?"

"That's when something climbs out of the pond," Kiana said.

"Or hops," Terezia added.

I then said, "I'm going to start reading now. Don't forget to hold up one of your cards for each sentence I read to show whether something is being added to or subtracted from the pond." As I read the book, each student held up one of the squares so that I could see everyone's response. The children could also see one another's responses, which helped them check their decisions.

We used the same format several other times during the year. On those occasions, rather than read *Splash!*, I read story problems from our math book. Again, to keep the focus on the operations used to solve each problem, I didn't ask students to figure the answer.

Questions and Discussion

▲ *Doesn't it confuse children to present addition and subtraction situations together?*

When children focus on only one operation at a time, they don't have to think about which words indicate a particular operation. In real life, addition and subtraction are not separated in this artificial way. This story gives students a reason to listen carefully and think about what's happening. It also gives them the opportunity to check themselves, since the illustration on every page shows which characters are in and out of the pond. The last activity reinforces children's understanding of the operations by allowing students to focus specifically on the operations without finding the total number of characters in the pond.

▲ *When you observe the children manipulating the tiles, what do you look for?*

I keep the following questions in mind as I observe the children:

- ▲ Do students count every tile each time they answer a question?
- ▲ Are they able to determine one more than a previous quantity without counting?
- ▲ Do students arrange their tiles on their papers in a way that facilitates easy counting?
- ▲ Are students confused when there is addition and subtraction action on the same page?

I use this informal assessment to guide my subsequent instructional decisions and to collect information about students that helps me decide when I need to provide individual attention.

CHAPTER SEVEN
COMPARING AND COMBINING

Overview

In this lesson, children learn to use playing cards to play several versions of the game of *Capture*. The games give students experience with counting, comparing numbers, using the concepts of greater than and less than, adding quantities, and finding differences between quantities. Repeated opportunities to play the games help children develop fluency with arithmetic thinking as they encounter the same numbers again and again. Also, experience with the games over time, and class discussions about strategies for figuring, helps children internalize combinations and relationships.

Materials

▲ playing cards, 1 deck per pair of students, with face cards and jokers removed
▲ optional: demonstration playing cards, large enough for children to be able to see them from a distance

Time

▲ one class period for children to explore and learn about cards, then time for repeated playing, approximately thirty minutes per game

Teaching Directions

1. Introduce playing cards to the class. Ask students to share what they already know or what they notice about a deck of cards. Be sure to point out the suits, the names and the values of the cards, and how to shuffle and deal cards.

2. The next day, teach the class how to play *Capture*. First be sure that each pair of children has a deck of cards with the face cards and jokers removed. Then model the game with a student, explaining the rules as you do so.

Rules for *Capture*

1. The dealer shuffles the cards and deals them one at a time, starting with his or her partner. Players place their cards in a pile facedown in front of them.

2. Each player takes the top card off his or her pile, turns it faceup, and announces its value.

3. The player with the card that has the greater number says, "_____ (the value of his or her card) is greater than _____ (the value of his or her opponent's card)," and takes both cards, creating a new capture pile.

4. If players turn over cards of equal value, each player turns another card up. Then the player with the greater number showing wins that round and must make a statement about the value of the last cards played, for example, "Seven is greater than two."

5. Play continues until players have used all the cards in their original piles.

6. The winner is the player with the most cards in his or her capture pile.

3. When children understand how to play, teach the variation *Double Capture*. Explain that the rules are the same, except that children turn over two cards instead of one for each round. They add the numbers that show on the two cards and the child with the greater sum wins that round.

4. After children have played both games for a while, lead a class discussion in which children explain their strategies for combining numbers. Show them two cards from a deck and ask for all the different ways they can think of to add the numbers. Discussions like this from time to time give children experience explaining their strategies for adding and hearing the strategies of others.

5. See the "Extensions" section on page 54 for versions that give children experience finding the difference between numbers.

Teaching Notes

Playing games in the classroom is a great way to provide practice with skills and concepts that have already been developed in whole-class lessons. Games provide a motivating reason for the practice, and games played with partners provide an accuracy check that isn't available when children work alone.

In choosing games to use in my classroom, I look for games that are fun to play as well as educational. They need to have fairly easy directions but enough complexity to be interesting to the children. Also, games must be easily adaptable to a wide range of abilities. *Capture* is similar the game of War, a card game that many first graders learn at home before they come to school. Because some children know the basic directions, it's a good first game to teach.

It's useful for children to have easy access to the playing cards. I keep decks of cards on the math shelf within easy reach. After I've introduced a game, children are able to play it when they have a few minutes at the beginning of the day or when they finish an assignment.

Children gain several advantages from playing a game repeatedly. The more comfortable they are with the rules and the procedures of the game, the more they can concentrate on the mathematics in the game. It sometimes takes several games for children to attain a good awareness of the mathematics they are using. A class discussion or a conversation with a group playing a game can also help students focus on the mathematics involved.

The Lesson

▲▲

DAY 1

To introduce the playing cards to the class, I began this lesson by finding out what the children already knew about playing cards.

"Have any of you played cards at home?" I asked. Hands went up and lots of children nodded.

"My grandma taught me to play Go Fish," Terezia said.

"Me and my brothers play War," Michael added.

"What do you know about playing cards?" I continued.

Sarah answered, "Some are red and some are black," she said.

"They have numbers on them," Kiana said.

Alisa disagreed. "Not all of them," she said. "Some are kings and queens."

"You're both right," I said. "Some of the cards have numbers and some have faces—the kings, the queens, and the jacks. Because they show faces, they are known as face cards. And because most of the cards have numbers, many of the games we play with them are mathematical games."

I distributed a deck of cards to each pair of children and instructed them, "Take a look at your deck of cards and see what else you notice about them." I gave the students a few minutes to go through the cards and talk with their partners about things they noticed. Then I asked for their attention again.

"What did you notice about the cards as you looked at them together?" I asked.

Crystal said, "You can turn the card this way or upside down and you can still read the number."

Lori, who was sitting with Crystal, said, "It works for the faces, too. No matter how you hold it, one face is right side up and the one on the bottom is upside down."

"There's this funny card," Christopher said, holding up the joker. Several others had found it and those who hadn't began to search.

"It's the joker. It's an extra card," Mickey said knowledgeably.

Jacob said, "Antoine and I noticed that if you count the hearts in the middle of the card, it's the same as the number in the corner." Heads dipped as other children counted to verify Antoine and Jacob's discovery.

"Hey, it works for the diamonds, too!" Ace said.

I drew a heart and a diamond on the board and said, "Each of the different symbols you see in a deck of cards is called a suit. One suit is hearts and another is diamonds, and both of these suits always are red."

I then drew a club and a spade on the board and labeled them. "Every deck of cards has four suits, two red and two black," I said. "The black suits are clubs and spades, like these."

"Hey! There's no number one in these cards. There's a two and a three and all the other numbers, but no one!" Lori exclaimed.

Mickey explained, "The ace is really the one. My mom told me. We play cards all the time at home. See, it has one picture on the card with the A." Mickey held up the ace of diamonds and pointed to the diamond in the center.

I then said, "I'm going to give you some time now to explore the cards, but first listen to the directions about what you are to do. Start by taking out all the face cards; we won't be using them for today's game. Then separate the cards into suits so that all the hearts are together, all the clubs are together, and the same for the diamonds and the spades. When you've separated the cards this way, then each of you takes one red suit and one black suit and puts the cards in order from least to greatest." Sequencing the cards is a good way for students to become familiar with the deck and also gives them practice putting numbers in order.

Before I let them begin, I asked, "Who can explain what you are to do now?" I let several volunteers repeat the directions I gave. Then, for most of the rest of the period, I let them examine their decks of cards.

I interrupted the children before the end of class to talk a bit more about the cards. "If you take out the face cards, how many hearts do you have?" I asked to begin a discussion.

"Ten," Jacob answered. Others nodded.

"There are ten diamonds, too," Lori said.

"They all have ten. They all go from one to ten," Ace added.

"So without the face cards there are ten hearts, ten diamonds, ten clubs, and ten spades. How many cards does that make altogether? How much is ten and ten and ten and ten?" I waited until the children had time to think and then asked the class to say the total together quietly.

I then said, "When I teach you a game tomorrow, you and your partner will use these decks of forty cards. But a full deck has more because we include the face cards, too."

"And the jokers," Michael added. I said, "Yes, there are jokers, but we really don't use them for most games. But a lot of games also use the face cards. How many face cards are there? With your partner, figure this out."

Most of the children counted the face cards one by one. Some sorted them into jacks, queens, and kings—three groups with four in each. Others sorted them into suits—four groups with three in each. I pointed out to the children that whether we count them by ones or group them in different ways and then count, we always get the same answer of twelve face cards.

"There are fifty-two cards altogether," Kiana said. I nodded.

There are many standard conventions of card playing that students may not have learned yet, and I took the remaining time to explain some of them. I showed the class a way to shuffle the cards, by placing them facedown on a desk and swirling them around with my hands. This mixes them well and is much easier for small hands than traditional shuffling. Then I demonstrated the normal card shuffling technique; there are always some students motivated to master it. Also, sometimes children have difficulty distinguishing which symbols on a card they are to count to determine its value. Some styles of playing cards lend themselves to counting the symbols more than others do. If children are having difficulty, I use a marker to draw a box around the center symbols on each number card in the deck.

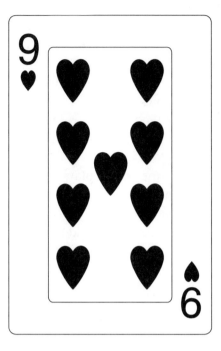

DAY 2

I began today's class by introducing the game of *Capture*. There are several versions of this game, and since it was the beginning of the year, I introduced a version that focused only on comparing quantities and the concepts of greater than and less than. In this game, children compare numbers less than eleven. From playing, they learn to recognize instantly how numbers relate to one another. For example, they begin to see that six is less than eight but more than three.

I said to the class, "Today we're going to play the game of *Capture*. You and your partner should have a deck of cards with the face cards and jokers removed. I'll give you a minute to remove the face cards and jokers, shuffle the rest of the cards, and pick them up again. One of you should hold all of the cards facedown. When you've all done

this, I'll teach you how to play." I watched as the children shuffled the cards and picked them up again. Some children had difficulty picking the cards up after shuffling them. Jacob was picking the cards up one at a time, turning them over as he did so, so they all faced up. I bent down and showed him how to gather the cards in a pile, pick them up, and tap the pile on the desk to even them out.

Next I instructed the students how to deal the cards for this game. I demonstrated and explained, "If you're holding the cards, then you deal them out. First you give a card to your partner, then one to yourself, and then another to your partner, and then another to you. Continue dealing out the cards one at a time until you've used up the entire deck. Then each of you should straighten your cards into a neat pile in front of you, facedown." I completed demonstrating and then gave time for the children to deal their cards. Then I asked for the students' attention again.

I invited Christopher to join me and said, "I'm going to pretend that I'm playing with Christopher. Each of us turns over the top card from our own pile." Christopher and I each did this.

I continued, "Then we each say our number out loud. Mine is nine."

Christopher said, "Mine is a two."

I then said, "My number is greater, so I say, 'Nine is greater than two, so I win this round.' Then I capture the cards." I picked up the two cards and put them in another pile to the side. "I don't want to get the cards I capture mixed up with the cards I was dealt," I explained.

Christopher and I then played again. This time he turned over a 7 and I turned over a 6.

"They're almost the same!" Lori exclaimed.

"Christopher has more," Jacob added.

I said to Christopher, "Since you have the greater number, then you have to say a sentence that tells what happened this round. Use our numbers in your sentence."

Christopher said, "I have seven and you have six, so I have more and I win." I nodded at Christopher to take the cards and start his capture pile.

I explained more about the rules. "If you both turn over cards with the same number, no one captures yet. Then you each have to turn over another card. Put the second card on top of the first one you turned over. Then the person with the larger number captures all four cards."

"This is just like War," Michael said.

"Yes," I acknowledged. "This first version of *Capture* is just like the game of War."

I then continued with the last of the directions. "Keep playing until you've used all of the cards you were dealt. Then see who has captured more cards, and he or she is the winner." I saw heads nodding and I could tell that the children were eager to get started.

Before they began to play, I said, "Remember that on each turn, you both say your number out loud, and then the person with the larger number should say a sentence, as Christopher and I did, to describe what happened."

The children began to play. I observed them to be sure that they all understood the rules. I stopped occasionally to question students. For example, I said to Ignacio and Jonas, "How do you determine who the winner is in each round?"

Jonas responded quickly, "Most of them are easy. Like if I have a ten and Ito has two, that's easy."

"They're all easy," Ignacio added.

Double Capture

When I felt sure that the students were comfortable playing *Capture*, I interrupted them and introduced another version of the game—*Double Capture*. "You shuffle and deal the cards the same as you do for *Capture*," I explained. "But in this game, you each turn over two cards at once and add the numbers that show. Then the player with the greater sum wins the round and gets to keep all four cards." I modeled playing a few rounds with Kiana. The children all seemed clear about the rules.

"You can return to playing now," I told the class.

"Which game do we play?" Antoine wanted to know.

"Try playing one game of *Double Capture*, and then you can decide which of the two games you'd like to play. You can play for the rest of math time today."

As I circulated, I noticed that some pairs preferred *Double Capture*, others chose to return to playing the first version, and some switched back and forth from one game to the other. This gave me information about which children weren't comfortable or confident with the extra step of adding the numbers on two cards. I encouraged these children to try *Double Capture* again, knowing the practice of combining quantities was just what they needed.

A Class Discussion

After playing both versions of the game on and off for a few days, I initiated a class discussion. I asked, "What do you think of *Double Capture*?"

Ignacio said, "It's harder when you have to add the numbers. You can't just look and tell who wins. You have to add first."

Crystal said, "Sometimes I had to think about it for a minute, but then I knew."

Christopher blurted out, "It's more fun than regular *Capture*."

"What do you mean, Christopher?" I asked.

"Well, you don't just know who wins every time," he answered. "You have to really think about it."

Chanell picked up where he left off. "Like if you get two numbers and your partner gets two numbers that are almost the same, you have to add to figure out who wins that round."

"Give me an example of that," I said.

This time Crystal responded. "When Chanell and I were playing, I got an eight and a seven and Chanell got a nine and a six, but we both had fifteen!"

"We had more ties in this game, too," Alisa agreed. "That's the fun part." Several students nodded and declared their agreement. "Then if you win, you get a *lot* of cards!" she said, smiling.

Crystal raised her hand. "I think *Double Capture* is hard sometimes. But sometimes it's easy."

"Why don't you give us an example of an easy round and a hard one, Crystal?" I suggested.

Crystal thought for a minute, looking at the ceiling. "If I get a five and a one, and Antoine gets a ten and another ten, that's easy. But if I get cards like Chanell and Christopher, that's hard!"

I then focused the children on strategies for adding. I took out my large demonstration playing cards. I find these very useful in teaching and talking about card games with the whole class. I held up the first two cards, a 7 and a 2. "How could you figure out the total of these two cards?" I asked.

Some hands shot right up in the air, but I waited a minute or so for other children who were still thinking about it. As the children realized I was waiting, more of them put up their hands. When almost all had done so, I called on Antoine.

"You go seven, eight, nine," he said, putting up fingers when he counted.

"I just knew the answer," Kiana said. "It's an easy one."

"I know that seven and three makes ten," Terezia said. "I know my tens. So seven and two makes nine."

No one offered another way, so I put those cards down and held up a 9 and a 6. Again, I waited to give children a chance to think. Waiting not only gives children the idea that I expect them to participate and think about the problem, but it also supports the notion that being quick isn't necessary, that it's fine to take time to reason. I called on Lori.

"You can just take one from the six and make the nine a ten. And then you'd have ten and five, and that's fifteen," she said.

"I know another way," Ace said. "You can start with nine and count on six more on your fingers." He demonstrated by saying, "Nine," and then showing fingers as he counted, "ten, eleven, twelve, thirteen, fourteen, fifteen."

"Does anyone have another way?" I asked. No one volunteered, so I pulled the next two cards off the top of the deck, an 8 and a 2. "How would you find the total of these two cards?" I asked.

"That's easy! It's ten," Terezia exclaimed, again demonstrating her confidence with numbers that add up to ten.

"What if you didn't know your tens yet?" I asked. "Is there another way you could find the sum?"

"Sure," Ace replied. "You could just count on, like I did last time. Eight, nine, ten."

The next two cards I turned over were a 6 and a 5. Hands went up immediately. I called on Kiana.

"There's two ways to do it," she said. "You could add five plus five, and then add one more because six is one more than five. Or you can add six and six, and take one away. But the answer is eleven either way."

We went through a few more pairs of cards, talking about doubles, making ten, and counting on. Some children participated more than others in the discussion, but I think that all benefited from hearing the addition strategies described.

EXTENSIONS

Two other variations of *Capture* are suitable when children are ready for finding the difference between numbers: *Difference Capture* and *Double Difference Capture*. In one version, each player turns over a card and the players find the difference between the two numbers. Then the player with the larger number puts both cards in a capture pile *and* takes beans or counters to represent the difference between the cards. The winner of the game is the player with the most counters at the end of the game. It's interesting to see children realize that the player with the most cards might not be the winner. They begin to look at the size of the differences rather than just the number of cards in their piles. They begin to notice not just which number is larger than another, but how much larger.

This game can be made more challenging if the children turn over two cards each time, as they did for *Double Capture*. They first add the numbers showing and then find the difference between their sums. The player with the larger sum takes the difference in beans or counters and captures the cards. The winner is the player with the most counters at the end of the game.

Questions and Discussion

▲▲▲

▲ *How do you know if your students are really learning something or are just playing a game?*

As I walk around watching children play, I check to be sure they are saying which card is greater before they take it. In time, they won't need to say this, but to begin with it helps them focus on the mathematics in the game more than just taking the cards would. Sometimes I stop and talk to children as they play. I ask how they know who wins each round. The most mathematically important part of this game is the discussion you have afterward. This doesn't mean you have to have a discussion after every game children play. In fact, it helps if they have played several games with several partners before you have a class discussion so they will have many experiences to talk about.

▲ *How can you tell if children are ready to move on to* **Double Capture?**

When students are confident and accurate with playing *Capture*, they are probably ready to play *Double Capture*. For some students, this will be on the same day that you first teach *Capture*; for others, it may take a few weeks of playing *Capture*. Sometimes I teach *Double Capture* to just a few students. The other students come to me asking if they can play *Double Capture* when they see their classmates playing it. The more that children play this and other games involving number combinations, the more they develop strategies for these combinations and begin to internalize them.

▲ *I find that my students don't understand what **difference** means. How do you handle this?*

I found the same to be true with my students, until I began teaching the games of *Difference Capture* and *Double Difference Capture*. When I introduce these games, most of the children aren't familiar with the mathematical meaning of *difference*. But once they learn how to play the games, which require them to compare two quantities to see how far apart they are, they connect the correct terminology to the concept. I find that children best learn vocabulary in the context of an activity that interests them.

CHAPTER EIGHT
MODELING SUBTRACTION

Overview

This autumn lesson gives children concrete experience with the take-away model of subtraction. Using leaves they collect and pictures of trees they draw, children first solve several subtraction problems and then create their own to solve. The lesson also helps children learn how to use number sentences to represent the problems they solve.

Materials

▲ 9-by-12-inch manila or other heavy paper, 1 sheet per student
▲ leaves collected outside, 12–20 per student

Time

▲ one or two class periods to accommodate twenty minutes for the tree drawing, thirty to forty-five minutes for the leaf hunt, and one hour for the subtraction lesson

Teaching Directions

1. Distribute 9-by-12-inch manila or other heavy paper and ask students to each draw a picture of a tree with bare limbs.

2. Take the students on a walk around the school grounds or to a nearby park to collect fallen leaves. Instruct them to each collect at least twelve and no more than twenty leaves.

3. Back in the classroom, ask students to each place twelve leaves on the trees they drew. Then tell them to pretend that an autumn wind has come up and blown some of the leaves off the tree. Encourage them to blow on their papers. (When the children blow the leaves, expect some to scatter on the floor.)

4. Ask the students to count the leaves left on their trees and figure out how many they blew off. Have several children report their answers and explain their reasoning.

5. Repeat this experience, asking children to place eleven leaves on their trees and then blow off some leaves. Before they figure out how many blew off, ask the class: "What kind of mathematical action is taking place when you blow some leaves off your tree?" Identify that this is a subtraction situation.

6. Ask a child to report how many leaves are left on his or her tree. Use that information to model how to record and explain a number sentence. For example, if a child reports he has four leaves left, then you write: $11 - \Box = 4$. Explain that the box represents the unknown number that they have to figure out. Ask children for the answer and have several explain how they figured. Write the answer in the box.

7. Repeat Step 6 for several other children.

8. Pose another problem for the class. This time they start with thirteen leaves and again blow some off. They each write a number sentence to show what happened and figure out how many leaves blew off. Discuss their results.

9. Finally, ask the children to do one more problem, choosing any number of leaves on the tree to start. Have each blow some leaves off, then glue down the ones left on the tree, and finally, glue down the ones he or she blew off at the bottom of the tree. Again, each student should write a number sentence and figure out the number of leaves he or she blew off.

Teaching Notes

Fall arrives in late October or early November in Houston, Texas. Our fall doesn't provide the wonderful show of colors that states in the Northeast enjoy, but it still provides the opportunity to help first graders think about the change of seasons. Each year at this time, I take my class on a walk to collect leaves. One way we use the leaves back in the classroom is to think about subtraction. I use the context of leaves falling from the trees to give children experience with the take-away model of subtraction.

While the lesson I've planned focuses on subtraction and the action of taking away, it's also an opportunity to help children see the relationship between the inverse operations of subtraction and addition. One way to figure the answer to a subtraction problem is by adding. For example, to figure how much ten minus four is, you can think about how many are left when you remove four from ten or how many you need to add on to four to get ten. It's valuable for children to become flexible and learn to think in both of these ways.

Another aspect of this lesson is the use of a box as a variable to represent an unknown in an equation. Using this notation gives children a beginning experience with algebraic representation. Although they will later learn to use letters to represent unknown quantities, using a box is appropriate for young children and just as valid.

While the subtraction lesson described relates to this specific context of autumn leaves, it should be repeated using other situations. For example, have children each draw a pond on a piece of 9-by-12-inch paper. Using cubes as frogs, they place the number of frogs you designate in the pond. Then they remove a handful, representing frogs that hopped out of the pond. They figure out how many cubes are in the handful by counting the number of cubes left in the pond. Or, give them each a dozen or so paper clips to represent ants. Ask them each to make a cave with one hand, and push some of the ants into the cave. Then, counting the number of paper clips left outside, they figure out how many ants went into the cave. You could also have them draw six circles on 9-by-12-inch paper to represent party cups and put one, two, or three counters in each to represent candies. Then tell them that each child at the party eats one candy, so they must remove one counter from each cup. They figure out how many candies are left. Another idea is to have each child use a 6-by-9-inch piece of green construction paper to represent a garden and colored cubes to represent flowers in the garden. After students remove several cubes from the garden, they count the remaining cubes and figure out how many flowers were picked. In all of these situations, children have some concrete material to use to verify their thinking, you keep the focus on having them explain their reasoning for answers, and you connect the action to appropriate number sentences.

The Lesson

▲▲

Before taking my class for a leaf-collecting walk one day, I distributed 9-by-12-inch manila paper to each child. I said, "Before we go out to collect leaves, I'd like you each to draw a picture of a tree on your paper. Don't put any leaves on your tree. After we collect leaves on the playground, you'll arrange those on your trees."

When the children had drawn their trees, I gave one last direction before we went outside. "You should collect at least twelve leaves, but no more than twenty." Most of the leaves we found had stems, so they were easy to carry in a bunch.

When we returned to the classroom, I settled the children in their seats with their tree drawings on their desks and the leaves they had collected close beside. I said, "Take twelve leaves and arrange them on your tree." I waited for all of the children to do this.

I continued, "Now pretend that an autumn wind has come up and blown some of your leaves off the tree." The children happily blew some of their leaves off their

trees. Some fell on the floor, but most stayed on their desks.

"Listen to the problem you'll now solve," I said. "Count the leaves that are left on your tree, and then figure out how many leaves you blew off." The children lowered their heads to count the leaves left on their trees. Then some students tried to count the leaves scattered around them while others began to count on their fingers. Excited voices began to report answers.

"I blew off six leaves!" Misty announced.

"Eight!" Rodriguez exclaimed.

"All twelve!" Kurt said.

"I'm interested in hearing how you decided exactly how many leaves you blew off your tree," I explained.

Kurt spoke up first. "Mine was easy because I blew them all off!"

"What about you, Rick?" I said. "How did you know how many leaves you had blown off?"

He answered, "There were only two left, so I knew it had to be ten."

"I had to count," Chanell said. "I had five left, so I had to count to twelve."

"Tell us how you counted," I said.

"Like . . . five," Chanell said with her hand in a fist. She continued to count, "Six, seven, eight, nine, ten, eleven, twelve," unfolding one finger as she said each number. "That's seven."

I didn't continue having other children report. Instead, I used this first problem as an introduction. I find that whenever I ask the class to try something new, some students are confused. When they understand the mechanics of the activity and are comfortable with it, they can focus on the mathematics of the lesson.

I said, "OK, let's all try it again. This time, start by arranging eleven leaves on your tree." I waited until all of the children had done this.

I then said, "Now, along comes the wind again and blows some of the leaves away. This time, be sure that not all of your leaves blow away." The students all blew some leaves off their trees.

I continued, "Before you count the leaves that you blew off, watch as I write a number sentence that describes what has happened so far. You had eleven leaves to start with." I wrote *11* on the board.

"Mickey, do you know how many leaves you blew off?" I asked.

"I'm not sure," he said.

"Do you have more than eleven leaves or fewer than eleven leaves left?" I continued.

"Definitely less," he answered.

When I first start helping students make meaning of addition and subtraction, I find it useful to have them focus on comparing the magnitude of the answer they're looking for with the number they know. I do this simply by asking, "Will there be more or less than the number you started with?" This helps students focus on the actions of combining or separating and relate them to addition and subtraction.

I addressed the whole class. "What kind of mathematical action is taking place when you blow some leaves off your tree? Talk to the person next to you about what you think."

I knew that several children were already sure about this answer, but other children needed to think about it a bit. Asking children to talk to each other helps them clarify their thinking and gives them a chance to hear other ideas and modify their own. Also, talking to each other allows more children to speak at once and voice their opinions than a whole-class discussion allows.

Samantha reported for her and Jessica. "We think it's subtracting because there were some leaves and some got blown away," she said.

"We think that, too," Andres said. Aaron, who was sitting next to him, nodded. "Because we started with eleven leaves and now we have less," Andres added.

I wrote a minus sign after the 11. Then I pointed to the 11 and said, "You started with eleven leaves." I pointed to the minus sign and said, "Then you blew some off. But I'm not sure yet how many leaves you blew off. When we don't know what a number is, we can use a box instead. That tells me that there is a number in the sentence that is unknown that we have to figure out." I added a box to the number sentence:

$$11 - \Box$$

"Let's look at Mickey's tree again. How many leaves are still on your tree, Mickey?"

"Four," he answered.

I added = *4* to complete the number sentence on the board, then pointed to each part of the equation to explain what I had written. I pointed to the 11 and said, "So Mickey started with eleven leaves. Then he blew some off." I pointed to the minus sign to indicate the action. "But I don't know how many he blew off, so I drew a box." I pointed to the box I had drawn. "But I do know that after Mickey blew leaves off, what's left on his tree equals four leaves." I pointed to the = 4 I had written.

"How can we figure out how many leaves Mickey blew off his tree?" I then asked.

"It can't be five, because that would only make nine," Emily said.

"Ten would be too many," Aaron added.

"How do you know?" I asked.

"Because ten plus four is fourteen and we only started with eleven leaves," he replied.

"So the answer is between five and ten," Terezia observed.

"It's seven," Rick announced. "Six and four is ten, so seven and four is eleven. So it's really just like adding."

"Can you show us what you mean, Rick?" I asked.

Rick came to the front board and pointed to the box and the four. "These two numbers have to add to this," he said, pointing to the 11. I wrote a 7 in the box.

"So there are really two ways you could think about this," I said. "You might think, 'Eleven take away what is four?' or you might think, 'What plus four will equal eleven?'"

I repeated the same recording I had done for Mickey's problem for several other children. "Who had a different number of leaves left on the tree?" I asked. I called on Lauren.

"I had five left," she said.

"Watch as I record Lauren's story," I said. I wrote:

$$11 - \Box = 5$$

I explained, "Lauren started with eleven leaves on the tree. Then some blew away, but we don't know how many yet. But we do know that what's left on the tree after the others blew off equals five leaves."

Then I asked Lauren, "So how many blew off? What number should I write in the box?"

"I think it's six," she answered tentatively.

"Can you explain why you think that?" I asked. Lauren sat quietly, not sure how to proceed. I waited a moment and then said, "Would you like to ask someone for help?" Lauren nodded. Other hands shot up, and Lauren asked Emily.

Emily said, "Six and five is eleven. I know because five and five make ten, and that's one too little."

Andres had another way to explain. "You can count." He said, "Five," and then used his fingers to keep track as he counted up to eleven. "So it's six," he added. I wrote a 6 in the box.

"Did anyone have something different than four or five leaves left?" I asked. I called on Ace.

"I had one left, so I blew off ten," he said with confidence.

"Let me record your problem," I said. I wrote the number sentence, putting the 10 in the box to indicate Ace's solution:

$$11 - \boxed{10} = 1$$

"Does this number sentence describe what you did?" I asked Ace. He nodded.

"Can you explain?" I asked.

"I had eleven and the wind blew off ten leaves, so now there is only one," he said. I pointed to what I had written as Ace explained.

ANOTHER PROBLEM

To keep things interesting, I said, "Let's try another problem. This time, start with thirteen leaves and again blow some away. Then write a number sentence to show what you've done, and figure out the answer."

The students counted out thirteen leaves each and placed them on their trees.

When they were ready, they blew away some leaves and began gluing and writing. As pairs of students finished their recording, I had them explain their work to each other, describing the actions they did and how the number sentences they wrote represented their leaf stories.

As I circulated, I noticed that some students chose to record a subtraction sentence, as I had modeled. Others wrote an addition sentence, first writing the number of leaves that were left and then a box to indicate the missing addend. Either way was fine with me, as long as children recorded something that made sense to them. Seeing both representations helps children see the relationship between addition and subtraction, so I chose an example of each to talk about with the children.

I held up Michelle's paper with a subtraction sentence written as I had done. I said, "I can tell Michelle's story from the number sentence she wrote. There were thirteen leaves, and then Michelle blew some off. She didn't know how many she blew off, but she knew that there were five left. Then she figured out that she must have blown off eight leaves, so she wrote an eight in the box." Michelle nodded her agreement with my explanation. (See Figure 8–1.)*

Then I held up Aaron's paper. I said, "Hm, Aaron's sentence looks a little different. His starts with a seven, and that's too small a number to be the number of leaves before he blew any off. Oh, I know. After he blew off leaves, only seven were left on the tree. If you add on the number he blew off, you get the thirteen that were on the tree to start. So the number in the box, the six, tells me how many leaves Aaron blew off." Aaron nodded and grinned. (See Figure 8–2.)

---

* To make permanent records of their work, students used either precut leaf shapes or their own cutout leaves.

▲▲▲▲▲▲Figure 8–1 *The five leaves Michelle had left were easier to count than what she had blown off, so she recorded 13 – □ = 5 first, then went back and filled in the missing number, 8.*

▲▲▲▲▲▲Figure 8–2 *Aaron saw the leaf-blowing situation as an addition problem.*

ONE MORE PROBLEM

There was still time left in the period, so I asked for the children's attention and gave another direction. (If time were running short, I would have waited until the next day to do this rather than rush the children.) "Let's do one more leaf problem. This time you choose how many leaves are on the tree to start, but don't use more than twenty. Then you'll blow leaves off the tree. But this time, instead of blowing your leaves onto the floor, blow them just to the bottom of your page. Then glue down all the leaves. First glue those that are left on the tree, and then glue on the bottom of the paper the ones you blew off the tree. That way, we'll be able to see what happened. After you glue your leaves, write a number sentence to describe the mathematical action that took place." I knew those were a lot of directions at once, so I asked children to repeat them for the class.

"Mary Catherine, can you tell the class what to do first?" I asked.

She replied, "Start with some leaves on your tree. Count to see how many you have to start with."

"What next, Emily?"

"Then you blow some from your tree down to the ground. But not the real ground, only the ground under your tree," Emily said.

Aaron had his hand up. "Aaron, what's next?" I asked.

"Next you glue down the leaves and write a number sentence about it," he replied.

The children got busy placing leaves, then blowing them off. I circulated, watching them as they recorded their number sentences. Several children recorded number sentences starting with the number of leaves left on the tree, drawing a box for the missing addend, and completing the sentence with the number of leaves they had started with. Others were more comfortable writing subtraction sentences, so they first wrote the number of leaves they put on the tree, then

drew a box for how many blew off, and completed the sentence with how many were left. Figures 8–3 through 8–6 show how several students recorded their thinking.

▲▲▲▲▲▲Figure 8–3 *Mickey saw both the addition and the subtraction aspects of this problem.*

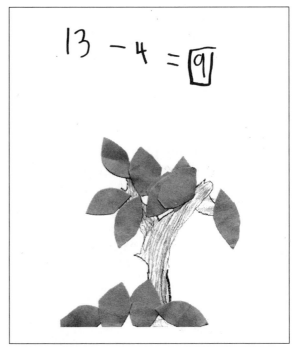

▲▲▲▲▲▲Figure 8–4 *Kiki recorded the four leaves she had blown off first.*

▲▲▲▲▲▲Figure 8–5 *To explain his thinking, Ignacio wrote 10 stay on, 2 fall off and included the number sentence 12 – 2 = 10.*

▲▲▲▲▲▲Figure 8–6 *Crystal had one leaf hanging on. She carefully counted the twelve she had blown off.*

Questions and Discussion

▲▲

▲ *What if the students didn't identify the action as subtraction? What would you do then?*

This wasn't the first subtraction experience for my class, but if it had been, I would have explained that when you take some away and are left with less than you had to start with, that means you are subtracting. I would show the children the social convention of using the minus sign and explain that one way to interpret it is as "take away." In this way, the experience would be appropriate as an introductory lesson. Keep in mind, however, that "take away" is not the only interpretation for subtraction. Figuring how many more you need to get to a particular quantity and comparing two quantities can also be represented as a subtraction sentence with the minus sign.

▲ *If you were trying to teach subtraction, why was it OK for the children to write addition number sentences?*

Both versions of number sentences are valid for describing the situation, even though one uses addition and one uses subtraction. I was pleased that the opportunity came up to point this out to the students. Just as we can use different words for the same story or situation when writing, it's okay to use different number sentences to describe the same story or situation in mathematical terms. I think it's important for children to learn that addition and subtraction are related and they can use whichever they'd like, as long as they can explain what they've recorded.

▲ **Wouldn't it be an easier start to tell the children how many leaves blew off the tree, have them remove these, and then count the number left?**

It would be fine to have children try some problems this way. Then the number sentence would be different. For example, if you started with twelve leaves and six blew off, you would write: $12 - 6 = \square$. Children benefit from problems like this as well. However, keep in mind that using the leaves and the trees is just one of many, many experiences children need with different kinds of subtraction situations. (See Chapters 5, 6, and 7 for other ideas.) And one special characteristic of this experience is that the children get to blow off the leaves, as a breeze might, and then see what results. This delights children. Also, the different number of leaves they blow off gives us a way to talk about different number combinations.

CHAPTER NINE
DAILY ROUTINES

Overview

Daily routines provide contexts that give children repeated opportunities to apply arithmetic skills to classroom situations. The routines help children see the usefulness of arithmetic as they develop the concept of using symbols to represent data and practice counting and computing in different ways. The children make decisions based on the data they collect and, later in the year, use number sentences to represent totals and differences. This lesson describes how to incorporate arithmetic instruction into daily classroom routines.

Materials

▲ none

Time

▲ fifteen to twenty minutes daily

Teaching Directions

1. Choose a classroom routine that will give the children the opportunity to collect numerical data, count, and compute—milk count, lunch count, book orders, who brought in field trip notices, and so on. See the "Teaching Notes" section for more suggestions.

2. Model using tally marks to collect information. Show the children how to use a cross tally mark to indicate groups of five. Model counting tallies both by ones and by using the groups of five.

3. As the year goes on, use the information collected for computational practice with addition and subtraction.

Teaching Notes

There are opportunities during every school day for children to use arithmetic as a tool, not just to answer questions posed by the teacher, but to keep records, solve problems, and bring meaning to routine situations that arise. Routines are extremely effective for helping children make sense of arithmetic and see its usefulness in their daily lives.

I've chosen the classroom routine of lunch count in the following vignette to provide a specific example of how to incorporate a routine into arithmetic instruction. What I've described models how I developed the use of the lunch counts over the school year. You'll need to adapt what I've presented to fit a routine from your own classroom. I use this routine because it's familiar to the children since we attend to it every day in my class, but the numbers fluctuate, varying the daily numerical experience. The example also models how to change the emphasis of an experience over the year. While I began with a focus on counting, later in the year as the children's learning progressed, I included more computation and less counting.

Examples of other classroom routines that are also suitable include taking attendance, sharing snacks, collecting milk money or money for book club orders, distributing paper or other materials that must be counted, and figuring out if you have enough of an item for everyone in the class to have a particular amount. Choose one or more to integrate into your yearlong instruction.

I describe the lessons here in the way I taught them, as short experiences lasting fifteen minutes or so. However, these experiences also have the potential to be used as full-blown lessons filling an entire math class and, at times, I've done just that.

The Lesson

▲▲▲

AT THE BEGINNING OF THE YEAR

At the start of every day at our elementary school, children who will be eating the school lunch choose one of two lunch entrees *or* a chef salad. Each class sends a count to the cafeteria manager indicating how many children will be eating each entree. I explained this routine to my class on the first day of school, and we talked about why the information was important to the cafeteria manager. Understanding the reason behind the daily task helps students understand the need for an accurate count.

One day near the beginning of the year, I said to the class, "Your choices for lunch today are a hamburger, chicken nuggets, or a salad." I recorded the entree choices on the board, asking students to suggest the letters to write as I slowly pronounced the words. In this way, I used the routine for a shared writing experience before beginning the arithmetic experience. I find that over the year, children develop fluency with the common words we use over and over—*hamburger, chicken, salad, pizza*, and so on. Later in the year, students take over the writing.

I then said, "If you want to eat a hamburger today for lunch, please stand up." When the students making this choice were standing, I began to call out their names, one at a time. As I said each name, I made a tally mark on the chalkboard next to the name of the entry.

After calling the third name and making the third tally mark, I asked the class, "What do you think these marks are for?" Some students realize right away that the marks stand for the names I call out, but other children need a good deal of exposure to this procedure before the representation makes sense to them.

As I called out the fifth name, I made a cross mark across the first four tallies to show a group of five. I explained, "The fifth tally mark always goes across the other four. This makes groups of five. Whenever you see that it's time to make a cross mark, we'll together say, 'Five.'" Even though I had already make a cross mark, I drew my finger over it and said aloud, "Five." I repeated this, and the children chimed in, "Five!"

On this day, six children chose chicken nuggets, three chose hamburgers, and two chose salads. When I had made tally marks for these choices, I said, "Now stand if you brought your lunch from home." Ten children stood, which gave us two opportunities to practice saying five when it was time for cross marks.

chicken nuggets	卅 /
hamburger	///
salad	//
lunch from home	卅 卅

When I had accounted for all twenty-one children, I asked my students to count with me. "Let's start with the chicken nuggets," I said. "Count with me as I point to each tally mark." The children counted with me to six as I pointed.

I then said, "It's always a good idea to check our counting. Now let's count another way, starting with this group of five we have." I circled the group of five with a

finger and said, "We know there are five marks here, so we can just say five when I point to it. So we count like this: five, six." I moved my finger to the last tally mark when I said "six."

"I'll do this again, and you count along with me," I said. We counted together, "Five, six."

I wrote the number 6 next to the tally marks.

Counting the tally marks for the hamburgers was simpler. "One, two, three" the children counted with me as I pointed to each tally. I repeated the counting to model checking our work and then recorded a 3. We counted the salads the same way and I recorded a 2.

For the lunches from home, we counted the tally marks as I had done for the chicken nuggets, first by ones and then by fives. I recorded a 10.

chicken nuggets	卅 /	6
hamburger	///	3
salad	//	2
lunch from home	卅 卅	10

Over the next weeks, I continued to count by ones and then by fives. Just because I tell the students that each group of four tallies with a slash mark across them makes a group of five, and model how to count by fives or to count on from five, I don't assume that all of children understand that there actually are five marks in each group. That's why I also have them count tally marks by ones. Gradually over the year, as students count many times, they learn how to count by making use of tallies grouped into fives, and they begin to use tally marks in this way on their own.

I then asked, "How can we be sure that everyone in the classroom has voted?"

"We could ask everybody," Rick suggested.

I responded, "Yes, we could do that, but is there a way we could tell by just looking at the data on the board?"

I noticed Lori looking around the room and counting. "Can you tell us what you're doing, Lori?" I asked.

"I'm counting to see how many kids there are in the class," she answered.

"How will that help you know if everyone has been counted?" I asked.

"Then we can count all the marks on the board and see if it's the same as the kids in the class," she responded.

Together we counted the children in the class and I recorded 21 on the board.

"Let's count the tally marks to see if I've made twenty-one of them," I said. As I pointed, the children counted them by ones. Then I modeled how to count by fives, circling the groups and counting, "Five, ten, fifteen," for the lunches from home and the chicken nuggets. I counted on the extra tally for chicken nuggets, "Sixteen." I continued with the hamburger tallies, "Seventeen, eighteen, nineteen." Finally I pointed to the salad tally marks and said, "Twenty, twenty-one."

On this day, the number of tally marks matched the number of children present. However, this doesn't always happen. Sometimes children can't make up their mind about what to have for lunch and don't stand for any of the choices. Sometimes children who brought lunch forget to stand or might not be listening. It's important for students to see that each tally mark on the board represents one child's vote.

A FEW WEEKS LATER

After about two weeks, I begin to model combining the numbers I've recorded to check the total. For example, on one day, the choices were soft tacos, a cheeseburger, and a salad. I wrote the choices on the board and quickly recorded the counts with tally marks. Then we counted the tally marks for each choice and I recorded the numbers.

soft tacos	///	3
cheeseburger	++++ ///	8
salad	//	2
lunch from home	++++ /	6

I said, "If we put all these numbers together, what number should we get?" We checked and found that there were nineteen children present.

I recorded an incomplete addition sentence on the board using the numbers and plus signs, saying as I did so, "Three people are having soft tacos, *and* eight people are having cheeseburgers, *and* two people are having salads, *and* five people brought their lunches from home."

$$3 + 8 + 2 + 6 =$$

I wrote a plus sign whenever I said "and," emphasizing the word each time. It's important for students to learn to associate the word *and* with the process of putting groups of things together as well as with the plus sign. It's helpful for children to hear the language of addition as they see the notation for it.

I then modeled for the children how to combine the numbers, adding them from left to right. A few students chimed in with me. "Three and eight makes eleven, two more is thirteen, and six more than thirteen is . . . fourteen, fifteen, sixteen, seventeen, eighteen, nineteen." I used my fingers as I counted on six more from eleven.

IN THE SECOND MONTH

As I continue with this routine, I keep an eye out when adding the numbers for particular numbers that are useful for extending the lesson, such as doubles or combinations of ten. Then I model how to look for and use these when adding groups of numbers.

For example, one day we had recorded the following choices:

spaghetti	卌	**5**
enchilada	卌	**5**
salad	///	**3**
lunch from home	卌 /	**6**

I also had recorded on the board:

$5 + 5 + 3 + 6 =$

I said, "I see two fives in this addition sentence. I know that five and five is ten, so I'll add those numbers together first." I drew lines down from each of the fives and wrote below:

$5 + 5 = 10$

I continued, "Now I'll add on the three; ten and three makes thirteen." I added to what I had recorded:

$5 + 5 = 10$
$10 + 3 = 13$

"Finally, I'll add on the six," I said. I modeled using my fingers to count on six from thirteen. I added to what I had recorded.

$5 + 5 = 10$
$10 + 3 = 13$
$13 + 6 = 19$

The more modeling I do in this informal way, the more students pick up on my strategies for adding and how I record. After a couple of weeks, I ask the students to identify any "easy" combinations they see in a number sentence. When I do this, I have to accept whatever they give me as an easy combination. What's easy and helpful to me, or to one student, may not be for another. For example, a student who "just

knows" that three and six makes nine might choose that to start with. It's important not to pass judgment on what the best strategies are. Later in the year, talk more about efficiency in adding strings of numbers, but for now I want to encourage children to think in ways that make sense to them, build their confidence, and help them see alternative approaches.

IN THE SPRING

This daily routine changes throughout the year, and the way it changes differs each year, depending on the particular strengths students bring to the classroom. One year, for example, we might spend a little longer counting individual tally marks than we do in another year.

Also, by this time in the year, I've typically transferred the responsibility for this daily routine to the children. Pairs of students now take charge of the lunch count. Each child is responsible for this task two days in a row. I have a classroom pocket job chart where I post the children's names, and when I decide to add lunch counts to our list of daily classroom jobs, I begin by choosing a child to work with me as the first pair. For example, in one class when I added this job to our rotating job chart, I said, "I've put Melony's name on the job chart to show that lunch count is her job today. There will always be two people doing this job, but just for today, I'll be Melony's partner. Tomorrow will be Melony's second day, and Rick will have the job as well. Then Melony will move on to the next job and Rick will stay for his second day of lunch count."

Another change I typically institute in the spring is the addition of a mystery number to the lunch count. The mystery number is the count for one of the lunch choices. For instance, one day, the choices were spaghetti, a chicken sandwich, and a salad. After writing all of the choices on the board,

I had students stand and be counted only for the chicken sandwich, the salad, or if they brought their lunches from home.

spaghetti		
chicken sandwich	⫫⫫ /	6
salad	/	1
lunch from home	⫫⫫ ///	8

Then we figured out the number of children present and I recorded on the board:

$\Box + 6 + 1 + 8 = 21$

"How many children do you think are choosing spaghetti today?" I asked. "Instead of asking them to stand up, how can we figure this out from the information we have?"

"All the numbers together have to equal twenty-one, right?" Rick said.

"Right," I added. "How can you use that information?"

"Well," he continued, "if we add six and one and eight, we get fifteen. Then it just takes five more to make twenty, and one more to make twenty-one."

"That's six more in all," Alisa added.

"So six goes in the box," Ace said. "Like if we started with fifteen and counted until we got to twenty-one, it would be six more."

I said, "Another way we could think about it is like this." I recorded on the board as I said, "Twenty-one children in all minus the fifteen we've already counted leaves six left who weren't counted yet" (21 − 15 = $\Box$). I added this subtraction model because young children seem to use addition more naturally. I wanted them to see that $\Box + 15 = 21$, can also be expressed as the subtraction problem, 21 − 15 = $\Box$.

Crystal had another idea. "We could just count the rest of the kids," she observed.

"You're right, we could. But the great thing about mathematics is that it lets us fig-ure things like this out, even if we don't have the people in the room to count."

After I've modeled this several times, the students in charge decide which item to use for the mystery number. When they figure out the mystery number, they decide if they want to check their answer by actually counting the children having the mystery item. This check is valuable, but after students become more confident in their calculations, they sometimes decide that they don't need to do it.

One day, Mickey and Sanjay were in charge of the lunch count. "Would everyone please give Mickey and Sanjay your attention for today's lunch count?" I asked. The two boys stood at the chalkboard ready to begin. They had already copied the entree choices from the flier posted near the board.

"If you are having burrito with cheese today, please stand up," Mickey began. As Mickey called out the names of the children standing, Sanjay made tally marks on the board and wrote the total next to the tally marks. Nine children chose the burrito entree.

"Our mystery number is going to be pizza today," Sanjay said. The boys went on to count one person eating salad and four children who brought their lunches from home. (Pizza is typically a popular choice.)

burrito with cheese	⫫⫫ ////	9
pizza		
salad	/	1
lunch from home	////	4

Sanjay said, "Next we add nine people having burritos with one person having a salad. That's ten. Then four more makes fourteen." Mickey nodded his agreement and recorded:

$9 + 1 = 10$
$10 + 4 = 14$

Sanjay went on. "We have twenty-three kids here today." Mickey recorded:

$23 - 14 =$

Sanjay reasoned, "Twenty-three take away ten is thirteen, and thirteen take away four is, well, thirteen take away three is ten, so one more makes nine."

Mickey then said, "I know another way. If it were twenty-three minus thirteen, the answer would be ten, but fourteen means take away one more, so it's nine."

As children listen to one another explain their addition and subtraction strategies daily, those strategies become public property. Children begin to try out one another's strategies and become comfortable computing in more than one way. As a class we talk about how some strategies are more efficient than others and which is the most efficient for a particular problem. These discussions shift the focus from finding many ways to solve a problem to finding efficient ways to solve a problem.

Questions and Discussion

▲▲▲

▲ How do you know when to turn the job over to your students?

Although it depends on the students in a given class, generally first graders are ready to take on this job after two or three months. They need to be able to read and write the menu without much help from you, and they need to understand the purpose and the use of tallies.

▲ What if I can't get to the routine every day?

In the beginning it helps to go through the activity every day to establish the routine and build familiarity with the procedure. There may be days when attending to the routine isn't possible, but I try to be consistent. I find it only takes a few minutes a day, and it strengthens the computational skills of my students a great deal. By hearing strategies explained and seeing them recorded again and again by different children, even a reluctant child becomes familiar with new ways to think and becomes confident enough to try something new.

CHAPTER TEN
FINDING MATH WHERE IT HAPPENS

Overview

In this lesson, children work together as a class to solve two problems: (1) *How much money is needed to buy fifty-cent snow cones for fifteen students who forgot to bring money?* (2) *How much change would there be from using a $10 bill to pay for all the snow cones?* The problems engage children with a real-world situation for which several strategies can be used to arrive at the solutions.

Materials

▲ none

Time

▲ one class period

Teaching Directions

1. Present two problems with a context similar to the snow cone problems.
2. Allow students to discuss possible solutions and talk through them together.
3. Provide manipulatives for students to use in acting out the problems.
4. Discuss the reasonableness of their solutions.

Teaching Notes

Helping children see the usefulness of mathematics in their everyday lives is an important part of teaching arithmetic. Children need to see both the utility and the inherent beauty of mathematics. As adults, we use arithmetic every day, often without thinking about it. If we share our thinking with young children, they will become aware of how necessary arithmetic is for solving problems and will see the purpose in learning it.

Some of the best arithmetic lessons arise from situations that occur in classrooms. I've described here one that happened in my classroom. At our school, during the warm months, the PTA sells snow cones one day a week as a fund-raiser. One week, I forgot to send home the PTA notes reminding parents to give their children money for the snow cones. Rather than penalize the children for my error, I offered to buy snow cones for those children who didn't have money. I gave the children the problem of figuring out how much that would cost and how much change I would get from a ten-dollar bill.

While this particular instance was a real one that arose in my classroom, I offer it because it's a suitable problem for you to present to your students and models for you how to use a problem like this with the entire class. However, there are many other situations that also lend themselves to the same kind of problem solving as this particular experience. Children can figure how much money it would take to buy every child in the class a carton of milk or a special treat. Given the price of pencils or erasers, children can figure out how much it would cost to buy one for each child. Planning for a class party or field trip can also provide arithmetic problems to solve. Whatever the problem, what's important is that children see arithmetic as a valuable tool for daily life.

The Lesson

▲▲

During the months when our PTA sells snow cones one day each week, we send home notes to families the day before reminding them to send money with their children. One week I forgot to send the notes home and my students came into the room very upset. They heard talk about snow cones on the school bus and realized they were going to miss out on this favorite recess snack. Of course, some of them had brought money. After all, they had been bringing money for snow cones every Thursday since the beginning of school. But there was much sadness in the classroom until I announced that I would buy a snow cone for everyone who had forgotten his or her money.

"Won't that cost a lot of money, Mrs. Sheffield?" Jaleesa asked.

"Do you have that much money?" Ricky inquired.

"Well, let's figure it out," I said. "What do I need to know to decide if I have enough money?"

Sergio raised his hand. "Well," he said slowly, "you don't need to buy one for everybody, because I brought my own money." I heard other children say, "Me too!" and "So did I!"

Jaleesa took over. "OK, everybody. Raise your hand if you brought your snow cone money." She counted hands and announced, "Four kids brought their money. So you only have to buy . . ." Jaleesa started counting on her fingers to figure how many students were left.

"Can someone state in words the problem Jaleesa is trying to figure out?" I asked.

Jamie responded, "Four kids brought money. How many kids didn't bring money?"

"What else do you need to know to solve that problem?" I continued.

This time Togo spoke. "This is like lunch count. If there are nineteen kids and four brought money, how many didn't? It's like 'How many don't want chicken nuggets?'" he said.

At this point the classroom was noisy and disorganized. Children were standing up, counting on fingers, talking to each other, and gesturing around the room. But mathematical thinking was going on, so I didn't stifle their enthusiasm. They were invested in the problem, and they were making connections to what they had learned in other situations. Even more, there would be terrific payoff for them for solving this problem.

As sometimes happens with teachable moments, this conversation didn't occur during the designated math time. But sometimes the best lessons occur outside of our well-written lesson plans. Being able to see the potential for exploration and learning in a situation is where the art of teaching comes in.

"I agree, Togo. This is similar to the problems we solve every day when we do the lunch count. Can you write a number sentence to show what you mean?"

Togo went to the board and wrote: $19 - 4 =$. He said, "Nineteen," then held up four fingers, one at a time, as he counted backward, "eighteen, seventeen, sixteen, fifteen."

"I know another way," Ann exclaimed. "If the nineteen were one bigger, and the four were one bigger, it would be twenty minus five, and that's easy." Because we had nineteen students in the class, we had done a good deal of computation involving nineteen and had used that strategy before. Ann was applying it to a new problem.

"What does the number fifteen tell us?" I asked. It's important to keep relating the context to the arithmetic calculation so that students stay connected to the real problem being solved.

Selena raised her hand. "Fifteen is the number of people without snow cone money."

I nodded. "Now what else do we need to know?" I asked.

Selena answered, "We still need to find out how much money it is for you to pay."

"Snow cones cost fifty cents each," Kris said. "So you have to pay fifteen fifty centses. That's, like, fifty plus fifty plus fifty plus fifty . . ." His voice trailed off as his hands stretched apart to show what a long problem that would be.

"I can write that!" Melissa exclaimed. She went to the board and started to write the long number sentence. The class helped her count the number of 50s as her number sentence grew longer and longer on the chalkboard. When Melissa was done, Gita went to the board and counted the 50s to be sure there were fifteen.

"Now what?" I asked.

Jamie raised his hand now. "Fifty cents and fifty cents is a dollar," he said, "so we can circle two fifties and make a dollar." Melissa began to circle pairs of 50s on the board. Above each circle she wrote $1.

As Melissa pointed to the circles, the class counted together, "One, two, three, four, five, six, seven dollars and fifty cents!"

Sergio raised his hand. "Do you have enough money, Mrs. Sheffield?" he asked.

I checked my wallet, found a ten-dollar bill, and held it up. I asked, "Will I get any change back?"

The whole class responded loudly with "Yes!"

Togo jumped up and said, "I have an idea!" He went to the front board and pointed to the circled pairs of numbers. "We can count backwards like this." He pointed to each 50 + 50 and said, "Nine dollars, eight, seven, six, five, four, three, and take away fifty cents is two fifty." Jaleesa nodded as he spoke, and I could tell she followed his reasoning. I wasn't sure about the others.

"Can you explain what you did, Togo?" I asked. He pointed again. "See, you just take away a dollar every time until you've done seven, then you take away fifty cents," he answered.

"Does anyone have another idea about how to take the seven fifty away from my ten dollars?" I then asked. Togo had offered a perfectly fine solution, but I wanted to be sure that the students knew that there were other ways to think about a problem like this.

Gita had another idea. She said, "Ten take away seven is three, so ten dollars take away seven dollars is three dollars. And three dollars take away fifty cents is two fifty."

We moved on to other things that day, not the least of which was snow cones for everyone in the class. During math time, I taught the lesson I had planned. But the minutes we spent talking about snow cones and money were important ones. Beyond the arithmetic strategies the students explained and practiced was the message that mathematics is useful and necessary.

Questions and Discussion

▲▲▲

▲ *When I have the children solve a problem like this, what should I be sure to emphasize?*

It's important to keep several things in mind. One is to keep reminding the children about the problem situation so that they continually relate the numerical calculations they do to the situation at hand. Another is to connect their thinking to correct mathematical symbolism, either by asking children to write number sentences or by modeling for the children how to do this. Also, be sure to ask children who offer solutions to explain their reasoning. Finally, each time a child gives a correct answer and explanation, be sure to ask, "Does someone have another idea?" Give all children who want to talk the chance to do so.

▲ *What do you do if a child gives an incorrect answer or an erroneous explanation?*

When a child offers a wrong idea, I don't jump in right away, but wait to give others a chance to respond. I've learned that when I let an error exist for a little while, it usually gets resolved through further conversation. Sometimes, the child who made the error notices it and makes a retraction. Of course, if no one notices, then I point out that the answer doesn't make sense to me, and I explain why. Then I give the children a chance to resolve the situation.

CHAPTER ELEVEN
MULTIPLE PROBLEM-SOLVING STRATEGIES

Overview

The children's book *Counting Crocodiles,* by Judy Sierra, gives students the opportunity to use patterns and a variety of addition strategies to solve two arithmetic problems. First the students figure out how many crocodiles are in the sea when they can see only their forty-two eyes. Then they figure out how many crocodiles there are altogether in the story.

Materials

▲ *Counting Crocodiles,* by Judy Sierra (San Diego: Harcourt Brace, 1997)
▲ cubes or other counters

Time

▲ one or two class periods

Teaching Directions

1. Show students the cover of the book *Counting Crocodiles* and talk about characters and setting. Have students make predictions about the plot.

2. Show the illustration on the first title page. Talk with the children about how they know that seeing two eyes means there is one crocodile.

3. Turn the page and show the full title page spread. Ask students to estimate the number of crocodiles in the sea. Count the eyes in the sea by twos and ask the children to think about how many crocodiles there are for forty-two eyes.

4. To help the children solve this problem, give them simpler problems and encourage them to look for patterns. Draw a vertical line on the board to make two columns. Label the left-hand column *Eyes* and record a 2 in it; label the right-hand column *Crocodiles* and record a 1.

Eyes	Crocodiles
2	1

Continue with four eyes and two crocodiles, then six eyes and three crocodiles, and so on down to sixteen eyes and eight crocodiles. Ask the children to think about the relationship between the pairs of numbers. Work together to determine that twenty-one crocodiles have forty-two eyes.

5. Read the book aloud. (If time is short, wait until the next day to read the book and continue with the lesson; don't rush through it.)

6. Ask students to figure out how many crocodiles the monkey counted. Before the students go to work, ask who has an idea about how they might go about solving the problem and explaining how they did it. Have all who are willing share their ideas.

7. After students have solved the problem, lead a discussion for them to share their solutions and talk about the strategies they used.

Teaching Notes

Counting Crocodiles, by Judy Sierra, is based on a Pan-Asian folktale in which a trickster animal, here a monkey, persuades crocodiles to form a bridge over water, under the pretext of counting them. In this version, Monkey lives on an island in the sea with nothing to eat except sour lemons. One day she spies a sweet banana tree on an island far in the distance. The problem is that between Monkey and the banana tree lies the treacherous Sillabobble Sea filled with many fearless, hungry, vicious crocodiles. One crusty crocodile boasts, "Why, head to tail, we'd reach across the sea!" The crocodiles line up, head to tail—one with a smile, two resting on rocks, three rocking in a box, four building with blocks, and so on up to ten crocodiles dressed like Goldilocks. Monkey counts them, skipping on their backs over to the banana tree island and then back with the bananas.

The combination of an engaging story, interesting illustrations, and wonderful vocabulary makes this a delightful book to share with any class. The mathematical element is not forced in any way but flows seamlessly from the story. The book provides two problem-solving opportunities for students. One comes from the illustration on the title page spread, which shows forty-two crocodile eyes in the sea; the children must figure out how many crocodiles there are. The second problem comes from the story; the children must figure out how many crocodiles made the bridge to the island with the banana tree.

The first problem involves students with the important mathematical idea that patterns can help us solve problems that are too big to grasp or solve with pictures. In this situation, the problem could actually be checked using a picture, which a skeptical student might want to do. Most children, however, will be satisfied with identifying the pattern and using it to figure the number of crocodiles there are if you see forty-two eyes.

The problem to be solved after reading the book involves students in cumulative addition, adding 1 + 2 + 3 and so on up to 10. There are patterns inherent in any sequence of consecutive numbers, making it an interesting problem to solve with lots of entry points for children. In any first-grade classroom there is a range of abilities, and this problem is appropriate for children at many levels of proficiency.

The Lesson

▲▲

I think it's important before reading aloud a book to ask the children to make predictions. This helps students invest in the story and have a purpose for listening. So before I began reading *Counting Crocodiles*, I read the title, showed the class the cover, and asked, "What do you think this book will be about?" The children focused on the crocodile, since his picture fills the cover of the book.

"It's going to count how much stuff he's going to eat," Ace predicted. "Everything he eats, he's going to count them," he added.

Terezia observed, "There's a monkey too, and a fox."

I opened the book to the first title page with an illustration of a pair of eyes in the sea. Then I showed the children the full title page spread that showed, on the left-hand page, many pairs of eyes in the sea. The children knew right away that each pair of eyes represented a crocodile.

"How many eyes are there in this sea?" I asked.

"We have to count them," Isaiah said.

"We could count them by twos," Ace suggested.

We counted together out loud and found out that there were forty-two eyes.

"So how many crocodiles are in the sea?" I asked. The children's initial response was to guess.

"I think it's fifteen," Melony said.

"I think thirty," Ace countered.

"Maybe it's twenty-five," Rick ventured.

"What if I told you that since we know that there are forty-two eyes in the sea, we could use that information to help us figure out how many crocodiles there are?" I said.

"Wow, that's a lot of crocodiles!" Christopher exclaimed.

"It is a lot of crocodiles," I agreed. "Would it be easier to figure out if there were fewer eyes?" I heard a chorus of agreement.

"Let's start with some simpler problems first and see if we can discover a pattern that will help us," I said. "How many crocodiles would there be if you saw just two eyes lurking in the waves?" I asked. I turned back to the initial title page that showed just a pair of eyes in the sea.

Lori answered, "There would be one crocodile."

"How do you know that?" I asked.

"Because a crocodile has two eyes," Lori answered.

I drew a line on the board to make two columns. I labeled the left-hand column *Eyes* and wrote a 2 in it, then labeled the right-hand column *Crocodiles* and wrote a 1 in it.

I then asked, "What if we had four eyes? How many crocodiles would there be?"

"Two," the class said in unison.

Eyes	Crocodiles
2	1

We continued recording pairs of numbers until we got to sixteen eyes and eight crocodiles. Below the 8 I wrote three dots in a vertical line. I put three dots below the 16 in the same way.

"I'm putting these dots to show that I'm leaving some numbers out," I explained.

Next, I wrote *42* in the Eyes column and a question mark in the Crocodiles column. "What patterns do you see on the chart?" I asked.

Eyes	Crocodiles
2	1
4	2
6	3
8	4
10	5
12	6
14	7
16	8
.	.
.	.
.	.
42	?

Kiana raised her hand. "The numbers on the eyes side are going by twos, but the crocodiles are going by ones."

First graders can often see patterns in numbers before they have the mathematical language to describe them. They also tend to see vertical patterns in charts like this, but what's happening between the horizontal pairs of numbers is often less apparent to them. I try to ask questions that will focus students on the relationship between the two numbers in each pair.

"What do you see happening between these pairs of numbers?" I asked, moving the side of my hand down the chart to indicate the number pairs. It took a minute for hands to start going up. I called on Jacob.

"I think the next numbers would be ten and five, because five crocodiles would have ten eyes. They all have a right eye and they all have a left eye. See?" Jacob blinked first one eye shut and then the other, to demonstrate his thinking.

Heads nodded around the room, but I could see some children didn't follow Jacob's thinking. "Can someone else explain the pattern?" I asked. Chanell raised her hand.

"If you start with the crocodiles it's like they're all doubles," she said. "Like two is one plus one, and four is two plus two."

"I get that, but there's another problem," Alisa broke in. "We don't know what number to double. We only know the forty-two."

"That's an important observation, Alisa," I said. "How can we figure out what number we could double to get forty-two?" I asked.

"We could just keep going down on the chart," Mickey suggested. "We could just keep writing until we get to forty-two and see what number we put in the Crocodiles column."

"I know an easier way," Christopher said. The class stopped to listen to him. In addition to being well-liked, Christopher was respected in the classroom for being good at explaining things in math. I noticed that children often went to him if they had a question about a problem they were working on.

Christopher said, "If it were forty eyes instead of forty-two, then it would be twenty crocodiles because twenty plus twenty is forty. And then there's only two eyes left, and one plus one equals two. So I think it's twenty-one crocodiles," he said.

"Oh, I get it," Terezia said. "Twenty is half of forty and one is half of two."

"How can we be sure that twenty-one is half of forty-two?" I asked.

"Twenty-one is how many crocodiles there are, because each one has two eyes—twenty-one right eyes and twenty-one left eyes," Melony explained.

"If we counted all the right eyes in the class, how many would we have?" I asked.

"That's easy! Eighteen!" Ace called out. I reminded him to raise his hand when he had something to say.

"So that means we have eighteen left eyes, too," Erik added.

"We have to add eighteen and eighteen to find out how many," Gerald said. I wrote $18 + 18 =$ on the board.

"Who knows a way to solve this problem?" I asked.

"My mom taught me how to do it this way," Terezia said. She came to the board and wrote the problem vertically. Then she used the standard algorithm to find the sum.

"Does anyone know a different way to solve this?" I asked.

Ann raised her hand. "I just look at the eighteens and see two tens. Eight and eight is sixteen so there's one more ten, and that's thirty. Then six more makes thirty-six."

"What does the thirty-six tell us?" I asked, bringing their attention back to the context.

"We have thirty-six eyes altogether," Ace said.

"Twenty-one plus twenty-one is forty-two," Kiana said. "Twenty and twenty is forty, and one and one is two."

"So you agree that there are twenty-one crocodiles in the sea?" I asked her, again showing the class the title page spread.

Now I was ready to move on to reading the book, but first we took a stretch break and walked to the restroom. (If time were too short, I would have waited until the next day to read the book and continue with the lesson so that I didn't rush through it.) Although the class was actively engaged in the discussion, there is a limit to the amount of "seat time" six- and seven-year-olds can handle.

READING THE STORY

When we sat back down and I began to read the book, students were delighted by the rollicking rhyme and the unusual vocabulary. They laughed out loud when the crocodiles said, "Later be our guest for lunch." We stopped at one point to talk about the meaning of *galore*, a word that wasn't part of their everyday vocabulary. It was obvious to the children that Monkey wasn't really interested in counting the crocodiles.

"She's just acting like she's counting," Ace observed.

When I finished the book, Christopher pointed his finger into the air and exclaimed, "There's a math problem here!"

"You're right, Christopher. What do you think it is?" I asked.

"How many crocodiles did the monkey count?" he responded.

"Right again!" Christopher presented the problem that I was just about to ask the children. "The problem you'll solve now is to figure out how many crocodiles stretched from Monkey's island to the island with the banana tree. But I want to know more than just the answer; I also want to know how you solve the problem. I'm interested in your thinking because I suspect there is more than one way to get the answer. Who has an idea about how you might go about solving this problem and explaining how you did it?"

"You could draw a picture," Antoine suggested.

"That would take too long. There are too many crocodiles," Alisa said.

"Everyone can make his or her own choice about whether or not to use pictures," I said. "What else could you use to solve the problem and explain your thinking?"

"You could write an addition problem," Terezia said.

Ace had another idea. "You might just write words to tell how you did it."

I said, "Those are all good ideas. You may choose your own strategy for solving the problem. You might want to talk to a friend about your idea, but each of you must write your own solution to the problem."

The students went to their seats and began to work. Some of them became totally absorbed in their own work immediately while others talked a bit before they began.

I watched as Kiki started making tally marks. She was grouping them by fives and labeling the groups in a cumulative count. I asked her how she knew those marks represented crocodiles.

"See, here's the first crocodile," she said and made one tally mark. "Then here are two more." Kiki made two more tally marks. "And then three more." Here she added one mark as she counted, "One," then crossed the group of four as she counted "Two," and began another group as she counted, "Three." I was interested to see how Kiki was imposing the structure of fives on her one-by-one counting of the crocodiles. She used the grouping to help her get the total

although she recorded each crocodile individually.

Alisa began at the end of the list of crocodiles by adding ten and nine. When she ran into additions she couldn't do in her head, she used her fingers. She recorded the running total as she went.

Megan's strategy was to use partial sums. She represented the crocodiles with tally marks, although she didn't group them by fives. As she added pairs of numbers, she wrote the sum out to the side. Then she grouped those sums in pairs to add. Megan got confused as she went along, so she worried that her final sum of ninety-five wasn't right. Next she moved to the other side of her tallies and again found sums of pairs of numbers. As she added this column of numbers, she looked for numbers that added to ten. Megan's method showed me that she had a strategy for finding sums of large numbers, but she wasn't yet able to keep track of all the numbers in an efficient way. (See Figure 11–1.)

When all the students were finished, I gathered them together for a discussion. I asked for volunteers to share their solutions

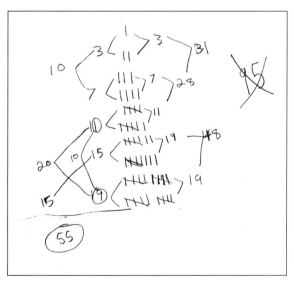

▲▲▲▲▲▲Figure 11–1 *Adding was a problem for Megan until she looked for sums of 10.*

and explain their thinking. Rick held up his paper and showed the class how he represented the crocodiles with tally marks. He indicated the marks on the last line and said, "This is ten already." Then, pointing to the arcs he drew on the side, he explained, "One and nine makes ten, and two and eight makes another ten." He continued pointing out the tens he had made and showed us the 5 left in the middle. On the other side of the paper, he had added the five 10s and the 5 to get 55. (See Figure 11–2.)

Ace showed how he had set up a series of addition problems, starting with 10 + 9 = 19 and continuing to 54 + 1 = 55.

As students shared their work, the whole class got the benefit of each student's thinking. They saw many different strategies and compared solutions. As they listened, those students who hadn't found the correct answer were able to take another look at their work and find where they went wrong. Figures 11–3 through 11–5 show how other students solved this problem.

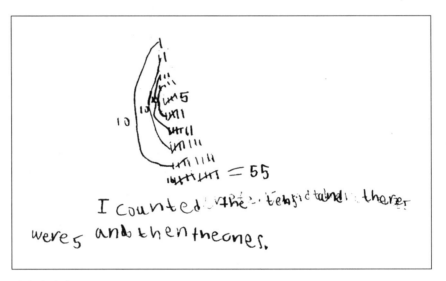

▲▲▲▲▲▲Figure 11–2   *Rick used the tally mark pattern to find combinations of 10.*

▲▲▲▲▲▲Figure 11–3   *Jonas started with tally marks but abandoned that idea for pictures.*

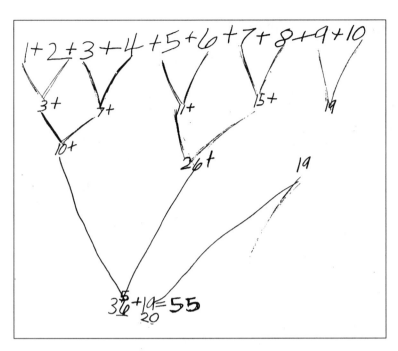

▲▲▲▲▲▲Figure 11–4   *Chanell demonstrated strong number sense when she shifted one from 36 to create an easier problem, 35 + 20 =.*

▲▲▲▲▲▲Figure 11–5   *Although Antoine correctly modeled the problem with tallies, he made a mistake when counting.*

Questions and Discussion

▲▲▲

▲ *What do you do when a child gives an idea that the others don't understand, like Jacob and Christian did in your class?*

I don't worry when all my students don't come to the same understanding at the same time. I know that children come to understanding in their own ways and on their own learning schedules. A great deal of conversation and different explanations are often necessary to provide children the chance to see things in new and different ways.

▲ *Do you correct the children's written work and return it to them? How do you keep track of which students are and aren't learning?*

It's important for me to keep track of students' understanding and skills, and I do this in several ways. I observe them as they work, listen to what they say in class discussions, talk with them individually, and review their written work. I'm careful, however, to be sure to keep the emphasis of lessons on teaching, not testing. I want my students to be relaxed, willing to take risks and try new problems, and accepting of feedback. I tend not to mark their papers and return them; I've found that this doesn't support their learning. Rather, I use what I learn from their papers to guide me as I help them think about new ideas and tackle new problems.

CHAPTER TWELVE
HOW MANY FEET? HOW MANY TAILS?

Overview

The book *How Many Feet? How Many Tails?*, by Marilyn Burns, contains riddles for children to solve with answers that are all groups of animals. The clues given include the number of tails and feet the group of animals has altogether. Using the book as a read-aloud, the children think through the riddles together, make guesses, and check their guesses against the answers in the book.

Materials

▲ *How Many Feet? How Many Tails?*, by Marilyn Burns (New York: Scholastic, 1996)
▲ 30 interlocking cubes or other counters

Time

▲ one or two class periods to read and solve the riddles in the book; two class periods to write and illustrate riddles

Teaching Directions

1. Read the title of the book to the students and tell them that it's a book of riddles. Tell the children that they need to think about all the clues to figure out the answers.

2. Read the riddles one at a time to the class. Stop after each riddle and have the students talk about possible answers. Then have them look at the illustration with the riddle for extra clues. If it would be helpful, have them draw pictures or use manipulatives to help confirm the answers.

3. For the last several riddles, and to prepare the children for making up their own riddles, after you read each riddle, ask the children to draw a possible answer. List the clues on a chart as shown in the following illustration. As children show their drawings, put a check mark if the clue fits and an X if the clue doesn't fit. Remind children that the answer must fit all of the clues.

	12 feet	3 tails	Sleeps under the porch
Five cats	X	X	✓

4. Over the next two days, have students work individually or with partners to create their own riddles. Instruct them first to draw a group of animals for the answer and then write clues. Give them each two sheets of drawing paper, one for the drawing of the answer and one for the clues. Paste them back-to-back.

5. Have students exchange and try to solve one another's riddles. Eventually, bind them into a book that children can check out and take home for their families to solve.

Teaching Notes

"What has four feet, two tails, and floats on the pond?" Two swans, of course! *How Many Feet? How Many Tails?* is a book of mathematical riddles easy enough for young children to read but rich enough to provide the basis for an arithmetic lesson. The book begins with Grandpa and two children walking through town. Each riddle is presented on a right-hand page with the answer on the following page. This allows children to think about the clues before reading or seeing the solution. The illustrations also provide clues, which help students make a correct guess when more than one solution is viable. For instance, in the illustration for the previous riddle, a swan is partially visible among the water plants in the pond. These riddles offer children the opportunity to think about numerical quantities in real-world contexts.

I've found that young children love riddles, especially when they can solve them by themselves. I've also found, however, that sometimes children give wild and unrealistic answers to riddles because they're not in the habit of thinking through a set of clues. Because these riddles are simple and provide enough clues, children have the opportunity to apply their reasoning skills to solve them. In addition to reasoning, the students do a good deal of counting and also thinking about numbers as representing groups of objects, such as feet or tails. They count by twos and have many experiences with groups of four.

The Lesson

▲▲

DAY 1

I read the title *How Many Feet? How Many Tails?* to my class and told them it was a book of math riddles. They were excited to get started. I showed them the picture on the first page and read, "What has eight feet, two tails, and pulls a wagon?"

"I know! A horse!" Kurt exclaimed. "A horse pulls a wagon."

"Maybe it's a dog," Sarah speculated.

"I'll read the riddle again," I said. I know that it's difficult for first graders to hold all the parts of the riddle simultaneously in their minds while they try to think of things that will satisfy all of the elements. They need the requirements repeated often.

I reread the riddle and then asked them to think about Kurt's guess. "Does a horse have eight feet?"

They all answered together, "No."

"Who has a different guess?" I asked.

Togo raised his hand. "I think maybe two horses," he said. I gave the other students a few seconds to think about that. Several students nodded in agreement.

"Let's see," I said. "Do two horses have eight legs?" I knew that while most of my students knew that two horses had eight legs, others hadn't thought about it. Amala ran to get the plastic animals from the sorting boxes. She held up two horses and began counting. Other students joined in the counting and all were satisfied when they had counted eight legs.

Then Jasmine raised her hand. "There are two tails, too," she said. Amala pointed out the tails on the plastic horses.

I read the riddle one more time, "What has eight feet, two tails, and pulls a

wagon?" By now all of the students agreed that the answer to the riddle was two horses.

"Let's check to be really sure," I said. I read from the book, "What has eight feet?" I paused while students looked at the plastic animals and nodded. I continued, "Two tails?" There was more nodding. "And pulls a wagon?" By now they were all fully convinced that two horses was the correct answer. I turned the page to show the picture, and the children all cheered when they saw the two horses pulling a circus wagon.

I read the riddle on the next page, "What has twelve feet, three tails, and sits in a window?" The illustration shows Grandpa and the children in front of a pet store window. Above the window is a small sign with a picture of a rabbit on it. I knew that I didn't have any plastic animals that would help the children solve this problem. I also knew that the number of feet in this case was too large for some first graders to picture in their minds. The riddle would force them to think about how to take the number apart to make groups of legs. After I read the riddle, I closed the book and put it aside. I wanted the children to focus on the words and numbers rather than the picture clues.

De'Witt raised his hand first. "Some birds?" he guessed with an unsure voice.

"How many birds do you think there are?" I asked. De'Witt shrugged.

"Let's see what we know," I said. "What does the riddle tell us?"

"There are twelve legs," Fouzia said. She immediately began counting on her fingers and I heard her whisper, "Two, four, six, eight . . ." Jasmine and Togo began to count by twos as well. So did Ann and Sammye.

But as I scanned the class I could tell that several students didn't have a clue about how to think about this big number.

I let the children who were counting continue on their own and posed a question for the others. "Is there something in the room we could use to represent the twelve feet?"

"I know," Dil said excitedly. He hopped up and returned with a small basket of interlocking cubes. He counted out twelve cubes and snapped them together.

"Now what?" I asked.

"A bird has two feet, so we can unsnap two at a time," Sergio suggested. He helped Dil unsnap groups of two cubes, counting as they went, "One bird, two birds, three birds, four birds, five birds, six birds!"

"It's six birds, Mrs. Sheffield!" Dil said.

Christy raised her hand. "But there weren't six tails, so it can't be six birds," she said.

Dil looked at her, crestfallen. "Oh well," he said, "we'll have to start over."

"Not completely, Dil," I said. "We still know there are twelve feet. If the answer isn't an animal with two feet, what kind of animal could it be with a different number of feet?"

"How about an alligator?" Candy offered.

Sammye spoke up. "They have four feet."

Sergio and Dil got to work snapping the cubes into groups of four, while Fouzia, Togo, Jaleesa, Ann, and Sammye went back to counting on their fingers. Other children watched one group or the other work. At the same time, both groups came to the answer of three alligators. Ann reminded them to check the number of tails, and three alligators fit that clue as well.

I reread the riddle one more time and again showed the picture. This seemed to spark Serena to ask, "Do they have alligators at the pet shop?"

Dil responded, "Sure they do! I saw them at the mall with my mama." This declaration satisfied some of the class, but the seeds of doubt had been sown for others. I turned the page and showed the answer.

"Three bunnies," I read. A chorus of "Oh no!" went up as Pamela got on her knees and counted the legs in the illustration for the class.

Dil shook his head slowly and sagely intoned, "Better luck next time."

I then read the third riddle in the book, "What has zero feet, three tails, and lives in a bowl?"

"Fish!" Jasmine shouted, immediately clapping her hand over her mouth. I reminded the children to raise their hands to respond.

Dil made the next comment. "Mrs. Sheffield, this is tricky. Fish don't have tails."

Kurt raised his hand. "Fish have fins on the side." He thought for a moment and then said, "No, that's sharks."

I saw a light go on in Ann's face. She went to the bookshelf and got an emergent reader that was titled *Tails*. On the cover was a picture of a goldfish. That seemed to convince the children that fish have tails, and then it wasn't hard for them to figure out the answer to this riddle.

We solved three more riddles together that day. I put the book away when the students began to lose their focus and get squirmy. I was surprised that we hadn't gotten to all ten of the riddles, but I knew better than to push past their limit.

DAY 2

The next day I gathered the children in front of the rocker, asking them first to bring their small chalkboards and chalk. I planned to have them use their chalkboards to focus on a different problem-solving strategy. I picked up the book and the children were pleased, ready to tackle more riddles.

We solved the next riddle as we had done the others, and then I read the eighth one, "What has twelve feet, three tails, and sleeps under the porch?" This time I didn't ask for guesses. Instead, I asked students to draw their guesses on their chalkboards.

Many children drew only one animal. I reminded them to think about how many animals would be needed to have twelve feet. I looked around the group and saw that Jose had drawn one caterpillar with twelve feet. Jose is an ESL student who is just learning English. In addition to trying to hold the three clues in his head, he was struggling with translating the English into Spanish to fully understand them.

Sammye and Candy both drew three cats and Sammye wrote the number 3 next to the cats. Sarah drew six ants and looked very pleased with herself for thinking of it. Pamela drew one bug.

Fouzia and Ashley each drew six dogs, drawing them in a side view showing only two feet each. When I asked Fouzia how many feet a dog has, she looked down at her picture and said, "Two." This surprised me because I knew Fouzia was a bright, practical girl with her feet firmly planted in reality. Then I asked her how many feet Clifford the big red dog has.

Fouzia laughed and said, "Four." Without any more questioning from me, she drew more feet into her picture and erased three dogs. Ashley watched and did what Fouzia did.

While the children were drawing I made a simple chart on the board, drawing three columns and labeling them *12 feet*, *3 tails*, and *Sleeps under the porch*.

"Who has a guess to share?" I asked.

Togo held his chalkboard up. It showed five cats. On the left side of my chart I wrote *Five cats* and drew a horizontal line across the three columns.

"Let's count the feet to be sure," I suggested. Togo pointed as we all counted the feet on the cats. When we got to twenty, I pointed to the first column.

"Do five cats have twelve feet?" I asked. When the class responded "No," I wrote an X in that column. Next we checked the tails, and I put an X in this column as well. Five cats could sleep under the porch, so I put a check in the last column.

	12 feet	3 tails	Sleeps under the porch
Five cats	X	X	✓

Sammye tried next. She had guessed three cats. She counted the feet on her drawing and I put a check mark in the first column, next to her guess of three cats. After Sammye counted the tails, I put another check in the tails column. Sammye then pointed out that cats sometimes sleep under porches, so I put a check in the last column.

I said, "If we have a check in all three boxes, then we have a possible solution. All three conditions of the riddle must be met."

Austin wasn't convinced that three cats was the only solution. He showed his picture of two bees. We added it to our chart and counted the feet. I made a check in the first column. We counted the tails, and I had to mark an X in the second column. Austin said that once there were bees under his porch, so I marked a check in the last column.

	12 feet	3 tails	Sleeps under the porch
Five cats	X	X	✓
Three cats	✓	✓	✓
Two cats	✓	X	✓

"Is there an extra clue that could help us here?" I asked, showing the children the page from the book where the riddle appears.

Christy raised her hand. "In the picture there's a yellow sign that says 'Meow,'" she said.

I turned the page and read, "One mother cat and two kittens."

We used the same system for the last two riddles in the book, making charts with the clues and evaluating the guesses. Each chart gave the children a visual organizational tool to help them keep track of all the requirements in their minds as they worked on possible solutions.

I ended class by telling the children, "Tomorrow you'll have the chance to write your own riddles." The children were excited about this idea. Some began right away, writing their own riddles in their journals and exchanging them with friends at their tables.

DAYS 3 AND 4

The next day I talked to the students about writing their own riddles. "What does every riddle have to have?" I asked. Many hands went up and I called on Ann.

"Some clues!" she said.

"And an answer," Kurt interrupted.

"You're both right," I said. "Every riddle has clues and an answer."

"Can it just have one clue?" Serena asked.

"Well, let me think about that," I said. "Suppose I gave you one clue. Here's an example: What has four legs?"

Children called out lots of answers. "A horse." "A cow." "A cat."

Serena said, "You can't tell what the answer is unless you give another clue."

I said, "With one clue, there are many, many choices. It would be hard to guess. I think you need two or three clues to narrow down the choices to one answer. Keep that in mind as you write your own riddle. But I don't want you to start with the clues. Start with the answer, and draw a picture of it first. Draw it on drawing paper and use your markers to color it."

The children seemed to understand, so I continued with the instructions. "After you draw a picture of the answer, write a rough draft of your riddle in your journals. When I've checked your riddle and you've edited it, I'll give you another piece of drawing paper to write it on. Then we'll put the papers back-to-back so your riddle will be on one side and your answer on the other, just as they appear in the book." I showed the class again how each riddle in the book appeared on one side of a page with the answer on the other.

"Does anyone have a question?" I asked.

Sammye raised her hand. "Do we have to work with a partner?"

"No, you may work with a partner or choose to work alone if you'd rather," I answered.

There were no other questions, so the students got to work. I circulated, watching them draw and then write their riddles. Some had difficulty keeping to only three clues, but most followed the pattern of the riddles in the book. As they finished, I had students read their riddles to each other to be sure they could be solved. Occasionally the clues were so ambiguous that the listener couldn't solve the riddle after hearing all three clues, and the writer had to make revisions. The children continued working on their riddles the next day.

After all students had completed their riddles, they took turns standing up and reading them aloud to the class. Other students solved the riddles at their desks by using cubes for the clues about feet and tails. Then the writer showed the drawing of his or her answer. Finally, I took all the pages of riddles and put them together into a class book for children to check out and take home so their families could solve the riddles as well. Figures 12–1 through 12–4 show some of the riddles students came up with.

What has _12_ legs, three tails, and rolls in the mud?

three pig

▲▲▲▲▲▲Figure 12–1 *Jaleesa drew her picture first, then counted legs and tails.*

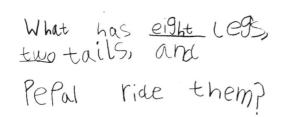

What has <u>eight</u> Legs, <u>two</u> tails, and PePal ride them?

two brown horse

▲▲▲▲▲▲Figure 12–2 *Ashley drew two animals and correctly recorded the answer, two brown horses.*

What has four legs, one! tails and has a baeb cow?

one cow

▲▲▲▲▲▲Figure 12–3 *This riddle had several possible answers until Christy added the final clue.*

What has four legs, zero tails, and etse pizza.

'he'
2 GIRLS

▲▲▲▲▲▲Figure 12–4 *Ellie was pleased with herself when she realized she could make her riddle about herself.*

Questions and Discussion

▲▲

▲ *I know children can easily become distracted by the animals and lose sight of the mathematics that is the focus of this activity. How do you deal with this?*

I think the questions I ask, as well as the comments I make, determine the focus of the lesson. When we are using a chart to determine if all the conditions of the clues have been met by a particular guess, I ask the students to think about where we've used a chart like this before in mathematics. Open-ended questions such as, "Does anyone have a different guess?" or "What could we use to represent this number of legs?" help draw their attention to the important mathematical ideas. As they work on their own riddles, I walk around and read their clues, reminding them if necessary to work out the numbers to be sure they lead to the animal groups they have chosen.

▲ *When a few children are working with the cubes, and only a few others are counting on their fingers, what do you do about the ones who aren't involved?*

I don't worry in a situation like this when some children seem to be observing rather than participating. Many children need to see a model of a problem-solving strategy in action before they are able to incorporate it into their personal repertoire. Just because a child isn't active doesn't mean she isn't participating by observing and thinking.

▲ **Won't children get discouraged when they offer a possible solution to a riddle that's not right?**

I also don't worry about my students becoming discouraged when they arrive at possible but incorrect answers. I know that when solving problems, we often follow leads down blind alleys before arriving at a correct conclusion. Students need to learn that persistence and perseverance are important skills in mathematics, as well as valuable life skills.

CHAPTER THIRTEEN
TALKING ABOUT NUMBERS

Overview

Conversations about numbers encourage children to think and talk about numbers in ways that makes sense to them. For a particular number, children may talk about its relative magnitude, how to take it apart into other numbers, what numbers they can put together to equal it, the importance of the number to their lives, and other special characteristics it has. Children's ideas stimulate the thinking of others, and the conversations help broaden children's own views about numbers in particular and in general.

Materials

▲ optional: chart paper

Time

▲ five to thirty minutes for each conversation

Teaching Directions

1. Ask students to tell you everything they know about a particular number. Begin with a number that is familiar to the children, such as five or ten.

2. If students have trouble getting started, try prompting conversation by pointing out something that you notice about the number. Then encourage the children to think about ways to construct the number or how they've used the number in their own lives.

3. If you wish, record the children's ideas on chart paper. Post the paper so that you can return to the discussion and add other ideas. When you record, model how to use words, numbers, and pictures to represent the children's ideas.

Teaching Notes

It's important for children to be comfortable reading numbers, writing them, comparing them, understanding their magnitude, and seeing how they can be composed and decomposed. Children who think flexibly about numbers see numbers as possible play-things and are better able to use them to solve problems and compute.

One way to support developing this understanding and flexibility is to spend time in class leading conversations about numbers. When first introducing this activity, I choose a familiar number, like five. Later on we talk about other numbers—ten, twenty, one-half, fifteen, and so on. In some years, children are particularly fascinated with large numbers and we have conversations about fifty, one hundred, and other large numbers. Other years, focusing on numbers less than twenty seems more helpful to the students. In general, I try to choose numbers that interest children and are landmark numbers, and I encourage children to think about the numbers in a variety of ways. In conversations like these, I don't worry about whether all of the children understand each idea that is offered. Rather, I see these conversations as open forums that allow children to contribute what they know and hear from others.

These conversations don't have to take a long time. They may happen in ten minutes while you wait to be called to the auditorium for an assembly. Or you may use them as five-minute discussions to lead off a math lesson. Sometimes I record the children's observations on the board or on chart paper, but more often our conversations are simply verbal exchanges that I try to keep playful and relaxed. Every time I lead a discussion, I'm surprised and often delighted by the things children notice about numbers. Also, I've found that the more discussions we have, the more deeply children seem to delve into numbers.

The Lesson

▲▲

TALKING ABOUT FIVE

"Tell me everything you know about the number five," I requested one day near the beginning of the school year (around the sixth week of school).

"It's an odd number," Christopher said.

"How do you know?" I asked.

"Well, if you count by twos, you don't say five, so it must be odd," Christopher explained.

"What kind of numbers do you say when you count by twos?" I continued.

"Even numbers," Chanell responded.

While Christopher and Chanell showed that they had some understanding about odd and even numbers, I knew that this wasn't so for all of the students. However, I wasn't concerned about this at that time. I knew that I would be teaching lessons to develop this understanding, so I merely accepted Christopher's and Chanell's ideas. (For suggestions about teaching odds and evens, see Chapter 14.)

I went on, "What else do you know about the number five?"

"Five is half of ten because five plus five is ten," Lori explained.

"We have five fingers," Christina added, showing us her hand.

Terezia said, "We can count by fives."

"Let's try this together," I said to the class. "Try to count along with me." I counted by fives up to forty.

I called on Kiana next. "You can make five with three and two," she said. I held up one hand, separating my fingers into a group of three and a group of two.

No one raised a hand to contribute more, so I ended the conversation and went on with the lesson I had prepared. I planned to have many more conversations like this, and this was a good introduction to how we would be talking about numbers throughout the year.

TALKING ABOUT TEN

On another day, I initiated a conversation about the number ten. I posted a sheet of chart paper and labeled it *What We Know About Ten.* Then I called on Terezia.

"Ten is a number we count by," Terezia said. Alisa, Kiana, and Terezia then demonstrated how to count by tens to one hundred. I recorded on the chart paper, and the children counted along as I recorded the numbers:

1. We can count by 10s: 10, 20, 30, 40, 50, 60, 70, 80, 90, 100

Rick then raised a hand. "Ten has a double, five and five." I struggled for a moment before recording Rick's idea. Although Rick's thinking was correct, his language wasn't accurate. I generally try to represent children's ideas exactly as they state them. When the language they use is incorrect or misleading, however, I represent their ideas in another way. When I do this, I always check with the children to make sure that

what I've written expresses what they were thinking.

In this instance, I wondered aloud, "Hm, let me think about how to write your idea, Rick." Then I wrote on the chart:

2. 5 + 5 = 10

"How about that?" I asked Rick.

"It's good," he replied. If Rick had looked puzzled, I would have asked him to tell me more about his idea, and then I would have tried a different way to record it. Rick's comment seemed to spark other students' thinking about ways to make ten.

Ace then said, "Six and four is ten, too."

"And seven and three," Melony added.

As I recorded their ideas, Sanjay and Melony suggested other combinations, and I added them as well:

3. There are many ways to make 10:
$6 + 4 = 10$
$7 + 3 = 10$
$8 + 2 = 10$
$9 + 1 = 10$

"Ten is even," Kirk then said. "You can count by twos to it." The children counted aloud by twos as I recorded:

4. Ten is even—2, 4, 6, 8, 10.

The list of addition combinations wasn't complete and Kirk's observation took us in a different direction. But rather than push the students to find all of the combinations at this time, I decided to keep letting children express their own ideas. However, sometimes what children offer gives me an idea for a lesson. In this instance, I thought about returning to the combinations I had recorded another time and extending the list to include all of the ways to represent ten as the sum of two addends. This would give me an opportunity to help children see that reversing the order of the addends also works, an informal way to discuss the commutative property of addition. Also, I wanted to have the children think of zero as one of the addends, something that hadn't yet come up, and use this as an informal way to discuss the zero property of addition.

"If you make a tower with ten cubes, then you can snap it and make two fives," Alisa observed.

I recorded her idea and pointed out, "That's how we can tell that ten is an even number. Any other comments?"

Terezia raised her hand. "Ten is a friendly number. Like, when we're adding, if you can get to ten, it's easier."

Lori then suggested, "Ten is important because you have ten fingers and ten toes." This seemed to strike a chord with the class and the children began to call out other situations from their lives that involved ten.

Mickey said, "My sister is ten years old, and I'll be ten in . . ." Mickey stopped to count on his fingers and then continued, ". . . in four years." He was smiling, excited to join the conversation. Several other students chimed in with their siblings' ages, and I called for their attention again.

"Who can think of another way we use the number ten?" I asked.

"Ten cents in a dime!" Kirk exclaimed.

"There are ten cards in each kind of cards, like diamonds, clubs, and hearts," Chanell said.

Rick disagreed. "What about the jack, the king, and the queen?" he asked.

Chanell responded, "Well, not counting those. I meant the ones with numbers."

I recorded Chanell's idea and then ended the conversation by saying to the children, "Be sure to tell me if you think of any other ideas we can add to the chart."

What We Know About Ten

1. We can count by 10s: 10, 20, 30, 40, 50, 60, 70, 80, 90, 100.
2. $5 + 5 = 10$.
3. There are many ways to make 10:
   $6 + 4 = 10$
   $7 + 3 = 10$
   $8 + 2 = 10$
   $9 + 1 = 10$
4. Ten is even—2, 4, 6, 8, 10.
5. You can snap a tower of ten cubes into two 5s.
6. Ten is a friendly number.
7. We have 10 fingers and 10 toes.
8. Mickey's sister is ten years old.
9. There are 10 cents in a dime.
10. There are 10 cards with numbers in each suit in the deck.

It seems that each conversation we have about numbers adds to the class's overall interest in them. I see individual children make connections about numbers, and I find that their sense about numbers increases. Also, they notice things we do with numbers in other areas of mathematics. Over time, students develop familiarity and become comfortable dealing with numbers, making them more confident when they use numbers to solve problems.

TALKING ABOUT ONE-HALF

I gathered the children on the rug one day to initiate a discussion about one-half. Talking about a common fraction gives me a way to sketch children's ideas, which models for them another way to represent their mathematical thinking.

I wrote *One-half* on the easel and asked, "Who can read this word?" Christopher read the word aloud.

"Who can write one-half as a number?" I asked. Lori came to the easel and wrote $\frac{1}{2}$.

"Who can give us an example of what one-half means?" I then asked. Several students raised their hands. I called on Christina first.

"You could have half an apple," she said.

"Or half a pizza," Kirk added.

"Or half a candy bar!" Kiana exclaimed.

"Hold on a minute," I said. "I want to draw a sketch of each idea."

I drew a quick picture of an apple and said, "If I wanted half of an apple I would have to cut it, wouldn't I?" The children nodded together.

Kiana explained. "You cut the apple this way," she said, indicating a vertical cut with her hand.

"How many pieces would we have?" I asked.

"Two," several children called out.

I drew a vertical line dividing the apple I had sketched and asked, "Which piece is half?"

"They both are," Rick answered. "That side is a half and the other side is half," he said, pointing to my sketch.

I pointed to the fraction Lori had written and asked, "What do you think the two in this number means?"

I called on Alisa. She said, "It means two pieces. Like when you cut the apple in half, you have two pieces."

"And what do you think the one means in one-half?" I continued.

"You get one piece, that's one-half," Lori explained.

I drew a circle on the easel to represent a pizza, divided it in half, and wrote $\frac{1}{2}$ in each half. I said, "What about half of a pizza? What does the one mean when we talk about one-half of a pizza?"

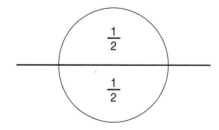

Ace said, "It still means one, but it would be bigger, 'cause half a pizza is bigger than half an apple."

"What about a candy bar?" I asked. I drew a rectangle to represent a candy bar, then a line to divide it into halves, and labeled each section.

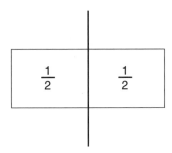

"The pizza half is still bigger," Ignacio said.

I explained, "Halves of different objects can be different sizes, but two halves of the same thing have to be the same size. Sharing something in halves means you each get a fair share, and the halves should be the same." This is an important concept about halves. Children often use *half* in a colloquial way and say, "Your half is bigger than my half." However, they have to learn that mathematically, two halves of something must be the same amount.

"Can you think of some other places you've seen the number one-half, or some other things you could have half of?" I asked.

"Sometimes we divide the class in half for a game in P.E.," Terezia said.

"Yes, we like to have the same number of children on each team, so the halves are the same," I said.

"My shoes are ten and a half," Jacob said. I wrote $10\frac{1}{2}$ on the easel to model for the children how to represent this number.

"What do you think ten and a half means when you're talking about shoe sizes?" I asked. This seemed to stump the class. No one raised a hand.

Then I asked, "What shoe size is just a little larger than ten and a half?"

Lori said, "I know, eleven." I wrote *11* just above $10\frac{1}{2}$.

Then I asked, "What shoe size is just smaller than ten and a half?" Several children answered, "Ten," and I wrote *10* under the $10\frac{1}{2}$.

"Ten and a half is halfway between ten and eleven, which means your foot has grown a little, but not a whole shoe size," I explained. "Can anyone think of something else that you'd like to share about the number one-half?"

"Sometimes my mom gives my sister and me cookies, and we have to share them so I get half and she gets half," Melony said.

"How many cookies does your mom give you?" I asked.

Melony answered, "Usually my mom gives us four cookies."

"And how many cookies is your half?" I asked.

"Usually it's two," she answered.

"Could half the cookies be more than two cookies?" I asked.

Christopher interrupted, "It depends how many cookies her mom gives her. Like if they got six cookies, then she gets three and her sister gets three." Melony nodded. I wrote on the easel using words, numbers, and sketches:

$\frac{1}{2}$ of 4 cookies is 2 cookies

$\frac{1}{2}$ of 6 cookies is 3 cookies

"What if Melony's mom gave her seven cookies to share with her sister?" I asked the class. I drew a row of seven circles to represent the cookies.

Antoine responded, "That's easy. They each get three, then they cut the last one in half and they each get one of those."

Terezia added, "They each get three and a half cookies."

I asked Terezia to come to the board and write three and a half as a numeral. I then drew a vertical line, cutting the middle circle in half and dividing the seven circles into two equal groups.

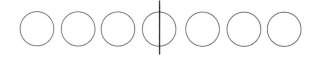

Next I explained a homework assignment related to our discussion. "At home tonight, have a conversation with someone about halves. See if you can come up with more ideas about one-half to add to our class list, and ask your families if they know of anymore places they've seen the number one-half. Bring your families' ideas back here and be ready to share them."

The information on the easel was an interesting record of our discussion. So that we could add their homework discoveries and other ideas at later dates, I transferred what I had recorded to a sheet of chart paper and posted it on the wall.

Questions and Discussion

▲▲▲

▲ *How do I know which numbers will start an interesting discussion?*

All numbers can start interesting discussions. When I choose a number for a discussion, I spend some time thinking about it myself. I give some thought not only to what I know about that number but also to what is particularly important about the number and how much I think a first grader might know and should learn. Also, even when I have something of particular importance in mind about a number, or a child brings up a particular characteristic, I don't worry about whether every child understands the idea. Rather, I use the conversations to open discussion and suggest thinking. Then, children's reactions help me make decisions about what further instruction I need to provide.

▲ *What if my students don't seem to know much about a particular number I choose?*

It rarely happens that no one has anything to say about a number. However, if the discussion is a total flop, just chalk it up to experience and move on. Another number might be more interesting, or perhaps the same number may spark a more interesting discussion later in the year. Sometimes it helps to tell the class something you've noticed about a number to jump-start a conversation. For example, "When I look at the number twenty-three, I think that it's twenty and three more." Or, "When I look at the number twenty-three, I think of twenty-three cents, and that makes me think of two dimes and three pennies." Or, "When I look at the number twenty-three, I think of the calendar. Today is the twenty-third day of the month."

▲ *How do you decide when to record the children's observations and when to just have the conversation?*

Since I fit this activity into odd times, more often I treat the conversations as incidental learning opportunities and merely talk with the children. However, occasionally I record their ideas, and I've found that there are several benefits of doing so. One benefit is that recording is a way to initiate revisits to numbers we've already discussed. For example, I might begin a conversation by posting a sheet of chart paper and saying, "When we talked about the number twenty-five, you had a lot of ideas. Let's try to remember them so I can write them down. Then we'll see if there are other ideas we can add." I leave the chart posted and tell the children, "If you think of any other ideas, let me know and I'll add them to our chart." In this way, we can revisit a number many times during the year, looking at it from new perspectives as new learning occurs.

Another benefit of recording is that I am able to model for children how to represent mathematical ideas. I try to incorporate words, numbers, and pictures in these descriptions, using as many of these ways as possible. Seeing my examples can introduce or reinforce for children how to represent numerical relationships with standard symbolic representations. Words and pictures help bring meaning to the mathematical representations.

CHAPTER FOURTEEN
EVENS AND ODDS

Overview

This lesson gives children experience investigating even and odd numbers. Children first work on the problem of figuring out how many children there are in half of the class. To solve this problem, they use interlocking cubes, building trains and seeing if they can break them into two equal trains to make halves. Using cubes gives children a way to test their thinking and verify their solutions. The children then investigate and sort all of the numbers from one to twenty and examine the patterns that emerge.

Materials

▲ interlocking cubes (Unifix, Multilink, or Snap cubes), enough for each child to have the same number of cubes as there are children in the class (at least 20)

Time

▲ one class period

Teaching Directions

1. Present a problem that requires students to figure out how many children are in half the class. For example: *If we divide the class into two teams, can we have the same number of children on each team?* Or: *If half of our class gets photos taken before lunch and half after lunch, how many will be in each group?* Or: *If the children in our class line up in pairs, will everyone have a partner?*

2. Distribute interlocking cubes and tell the students to each build a train with as many cubes as there are children in the class. If your class has an even number of students, ask them to include you as well so that their trains will have an odd number of cubes. Be sure that the students understand that each cube in their trains represents one person.

3. Ask the children to try to break their trains in half and to check that the two resulting trains are the same length. Reinforce that two halves of the same thing have to be the same amount.

4. After they've had time to experiment, talk with the children about why they can't divide the trains into halves. Ask them how many cubes they would need so that they could break their trains in half without a cube left over, and then have children verify that it's possible to divide that number in half.

5. Draw a vertical line on the board to make two columns. Label the left-hand column *Works* and the right-hand column *Doesn't Work*. Record the two numbers the children investigated in the correct columns.

6. Ask students to investigate numbers between ten and twenty, building trains and experimenting to find out if they can break them into two equal parts.

7. After all of the children have explored at least one number, ask children to report on the numbers they investigated. Record them on the board in the correct columns.

8. After you've recorded several numbers, ask: "Who can explain what we mean by '*Works*' and '*Doesn't Work*'?" Let several children offer their ideas.

9. Continue having children report and then ask them to experiment with numbers less than ten. This time, tell them to each make a prediction first before building a train and testing it. After they have had time to experiment, have them report their findings and add numbers to the chart. Do a quick check to be sure that you've recorded all of the numbers. If any are missing, have the children investigate them so you can add them to the chart.

10. Tell the children: "There's another label we could give to each of these columns." On the board, write *Even Numbers* above *Works* and *Odd Numbers* above *Doesn't Work*.

11. Ask children to each set up a chart on a piece of paper. As a class, reorder the numbers you wrote from least to greatest, and have children record them in order on their papers. Discuss the patterns they notice.

Teaching Notes

Many first-grade children have learned to count by twos, at least up to ten. Some have learned the chant "Two, four, six, eight, who do we appreciate." And some know that when things are the same, we often say that they are "even." However, most first graders have not thought about the relationship between these ideas and the properties of even numbers, or about the difference between even and odd numbers. This lesson helps develop the concept for children that a quantity is even if it can be divided into halves. It also helps them see the pattern that even numbers end with 0, 2, 4, 6, or 8, and odd numbers end with 1, 3, 5, 7, or 9.

This lesson is suitable both as an introductory experience for children about even and odd numbers and as an extension to reinforce children's prior learning. Using the class for the initial problem presents the mathematics in a context that is familiar to the children and helps them see how mathematics can relate to a real-world situation. Also, using the interlocking cubes provides children the opportunity to verify their thinking with physical objects, thus giving them a way to make an abstract concept about numbers concrete.

The Lesson

▲▲

Every year our school PTA has a schoolwide fund-raiser. One year, in order to get the children excited about the event, we held an assembly to introduce the sale. The PTA moms provided a prize for each class that was wrapped like a present. If at least half of the students in a class sold at least one item, the class would get to open the box and claim the prize.

When we returned to the classroom after the assembly, I put the box on top of the file cabinet. I asked the class, "If half of the children in our class have to sell one item, how many children need to participate?"

Hands shot up in the air and numbers flew around, but it was clear that there was disagreement about how many students constituted half the class. I decided to use interlocking cubes to help the children work out the answer.

I pulled containers of cubes off the shelf and put one at each table. I said, "Each of you needs nineteen cubes. Who knows why you need nineteen cubes?"

Christine answered tentatively, "Because there are nineteen of us?"

"What will each cube represent?" I asked.

"One kid," Christine responded.

I then gave the class directions. "Build a train with your nineteen cubes. Check with a friend to be sure your trains are the same size." I waited until all of the children had done this.

I then said, "Now break your train in half." When the children snapped their trains into two pieces, some thought that they had two equal trains. Their new trains appeared to be the same, and they didn't think to check by standing them up or laying them flat on the desk. Ace, however, held up his two pieces.

"I don't think this is right. They don't match," he said.

"Yeah, they're supposed to be the same," Alisa agreed, comparing her two trains.

"What do you mean by that?" I asked.

"It's like an apple," Rick explained. "If you cut it in half, you and your friend each get a part. But it has to be fair."

"So if you cut something in half, how many parts do you get?" I asked.

"Two!" they all said together.

"And what can you tell me about the two parts?" I continued.

"They are always the same," Sanjay replied.

"Equal," Christopher added.

"The question is, how many students are there in half our class?" I said. "How can the cubes help you find out?"

Kurt answered, "It's either eight or nine. One of the trains has eight and one has nine." Kurt had miscounted the cubes, but he was aware that the trains were one cube apart.

I said, "But if we break our train into halves, each has to be the same length.

How can you divide a train with nineteen cubes into halves?" Students tried over and over, snapping the cubes together and then separating them. Each time the result was unequal trains.

Finally, Chanell said, "I just don't think this is going to work. One train is always one cube taller. And the cubes are like children, so if we divide the class in half, we'll always have one person left over."

"It would work if we threw out one cube," Christopher suggested.

"It won't work!" Kiana cried in exasperation. "One of the trains is always bigger than the other one."

Since some of the students were becoming frustrated, I stopped their investigation for a few minutes of discussion. I asked the students to take their hands off the cubes and waited until they did so. I then said, "The reason this is difficult is that we can't cut a cube in half and put part of it on one train and part on the other train. But using cubes is still a good model for solving our problem about how many children make half the class because we can't divide a student up, either. For this problem, the best we can do is to say that half of our class is either nine or ten."

"Let's use nine!" Alisa exclaimed. "That way we'll have a better chance of getting to open the box!"

I then extended the question to have students use cubes to investigate dividing other whole numbers in half. I said, "Kiana said that nineteen doesn't work. Who knows what she means by that?"

Lori said, "She means you can't split it into two even trains."

"Do you know a number of cubes that a train could have so it *does* work to split it into halves?" I asked.

Chanell raised her hand. "If we got rid of a cube, we'd have eighteen, and that

works," she said. The children verified with the cubes that this was so. I went to the board and drew a vertical line to make two columns. I labeled the left-hand column *Works* and the other column *Doesn't Work*. I recorded 19 under Doesn't Work and 18 under Works.

Works	Doesn't Work
18	19

I got the children's attention and gave directions for further exploration. "You'll each choose a number between ten and twenty." Immediately, hands dove into the containers of cubes. I took a minute to call them back to attention and I waited until all hands were off the cubes.

Then I continued, "After you count out the cubes, make a train and try to break it in half. Be ready to report to the class the number you chose and if it belongs in the Works or Doesn't Work column."

The children went to work. Some unsnapped the cubes in their trains and then began over again to count out cubes. Some started with the train of nineteen and took some cubes away. When the early finishers raised their hands, I directed them to try another number, giving the slower workers time to complete an investigation.

When I saw that all of the children had explored at least one number, I called for their attention. Once again I had to remind them to keep their hands off the cubes while we discussed what they had found out. I called on several children to report on the numbers they had investigated, recording each number on the board in the correct column to indicate whether it could or couldn't be broken into two equal parts.

Works	Doesn't Work
18	19
10	11
20	13
16	
12	

After I had recorded six numbers, I focused the class on the labels of the columns. I asked, "Who can explain what we mean by 'Works' and 'Doesn't Work'?"

I waited until most of the children raised their hands and then called on Sanjay. "All the numbers that work, you can make two trains that are the same with them," he said.

Next I called on Terezia. "Those numbers," she said, indicating the Doesn't Work column, "all have a leftover cube when you try to break it into half, but the other ones work without a leftover."

Kiana added, "The ones that work make even trains, and the ones that don't work don't make even trains."

I continued asking children to report numbers until I had recorded all of the num-

bers from ten to twenty. Sometimes children reported a number that I had already recorded. In these cases, we used the information as a check.

Works	Doesn't Work
18	19
10	11
20	13
16	15
12	17
14	

I then asked the class to consider numbers less than ten, this time first making a prediction about whether or not the number would work and then building the train and snapping it in two. To begin, I asked the class, "Do you think six will work or not?"

Rick responded, "I think it will because I know that three and three is six." Some children agreed and others weren't sure.

I said, "When you make a prediction as Rick did, you can then test your prediction with the cubes. You'd build a train with six cubes and see if you could break it into halves."

I stopped the children from doing this immediately and gave the class one more direction. I said, "See what you can find out about numbers smaller than ten. Each time, make a prediction first, and then test your idea with the cubes." The children got busy again.

"All the doubles work!" Alisa exclaimed after a few minutes. "Three and three is six, and four and four is eight, and five and five is ten!"

Kiki looked up, puzzled, and then returned to building a train. Lori, however, stopped her building and looked at the chart. Then she looked at Alisa and said, *"All* the numbers on the Works side are doubles. See, there's eight and eight is sixteen, and six and six is twelve." Other students began to focus on the chart and Lori's comments. Ignacio nodded his head in agreement. Kurt took out some paper and began writing a list of addition equations for what Alisa had called doubles, with both addends the same in each equation. Others continued building trains and trying to break them in two.

After a few more minutes, I called the class back to attention again. I had students report the numbers they had investigated and I recorded them in the correct columns. I did a quick check to be sure that I had recorded all of the numbers.

Works	Doesn't Work
18	19
10	11
20	13
16	15
12	17
14	5
6	9
8	7
2	3
4	1

I then said, "There's another label we could give to each of these columns." On the board I wrote *Even Numbers* above Works and *Odd Numbers* above Doesn't Work.

"Do we have an even number of students in our class or an odd number?" I asked.

"An odd number!" was the resounding response.

"Can someone explain what you think even numbers are?" I asked.

Jacob volunteered. Speaking slowly and pointing to the chart, he said, "All the even numbers, you can make a train with them and then make two even trains, but the odd ones don't work." Heads nodded and children murmured their assent.

I now posed a related question. "What if we had nineteen cookies? Could we split them into two equal parts? Talk to your neighbor about what you think."

After a few minutes I asked for discussion. Kiana raised her hand. "Cookies are different," she said. "You can cut cookies in half, but you can't cut cubes."

REORDERING AND RECORDING

I asked each student to take out a piece of paper and a pencil, draw a line down the center of the paper, and label the left-hand column *Even Numbers* and the right-hand column *Odd Numbers*. I did this on the board and waited until they had all done so on their papers. One reason I wanted them to have the experience of recording the numbers themselves is that sometimes when they do the writing themselves, they notice patterns they missed when looking at the board. Also, this served as a model for organizing lists of numbers and gave them practice with forming the numerals correctly. Lastly, I thought having this record to take home might spark a conversation with their parents about the math they did in school that day. Having the papers in their hands would provide a starting point for this discussion and help them remember the mathematics involved.

"You'll each write down the numbers from each column, but we'll put the numbers in order from least to greatest. Let's do it together. What's the smallest number you see on the board in the Even Numbers column?" I asked.

They all responded, "Two," and I wrote it at the top of the new column I had labeled. The next larger number they found was 4, then 6, then 8. By now, many of the children noticed the pattern of counting by twos and they reported quickly, without searching. But since many of them were less confident counting by twos beyond ten or twelve, they slowed down a bit at that point. We ordered the numbers in the Odd column in the same way.

When we had ordered all of the numbers, I asked, "What patterns do you notice when you write the numbers this way?"

Rick raised his hand. "The even numbers go two, four, six, eight, then the numbers on the right side go zero, two, four, six, eight."

"And the odd numbers go one, three, five, seven, nine," Jacob said.

The underlying mathematics of even and odd numbers and their relation to doubles and halves is important to a first grader's growing number sense. While this investigation arose from a situation that occurred naturally in our classroom, the opportunity doesn't always come up. Still, I can provide the children the same opportunity by structuring the lesson around a different situation that calls for figuring out how many children are in half the class. For example, I might pose the following

problem: *If we divide the class into two teams, can we have the same number of children on each team?* Or: *If half of our class gets photos taken before lunch and half after lunch, how many will be in each group?* Or: *If the children in our class line up in pairs, will everyone have a partner?* Whatever the problem, I always use the cubes so that children have the chance to verify their thinking with physical objects.

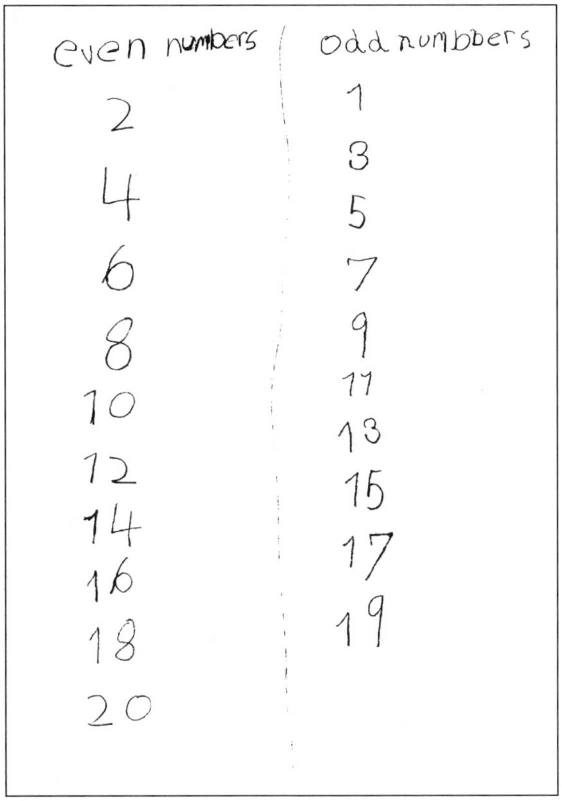

▲▲▲▲▲▲Figure 14–1 *Writing the numbers in order vertically gave students a different perspective and helped them see patterns.*

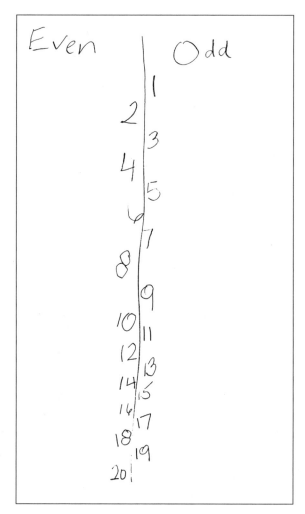

AAAAAAFigure 14–2 *Jaleesa wrote her numbers in order, alternating across the middle of the paper*

Questions and Discussion

▲▲

▲ *Even though Sanjay correctly answered the question about what 'Works' and 'Doesn't Work' meant, you still called on other children. Why is this important to do?*

It's valuable to have several students share their thinking about the same topic so that others can hear a variety of ways to express ideas about the same topic or question. It's difficult for some children to explain their mathematical thinking, even when they understand something well. They may not have been asked to explain their thinking before, or their understanding may be tenuous. Also, it's often difficult to follow someone else's thinking, particularly for young children caught up in their own ideas. Sometimes after listening to several explanations, a student finally gets it when that last child shares her thinking. Other times, it's the accumulation of all the explanations that finally makes sense to a child. Even for children who already understand a concept, hearing it discussed again or explaining it themselves helps them cement their understanding.

▲ **Why did you ask the students to investigate the numbers from 10 to 20 instead of first giving them the smaller numbers?**

I had two reasons. I'm always searching for activities that are accessible to all children as well as being a suitable challenge for those who are quicker, more interested, or more capable. Assigning the numbers from ten to twenty accomplished this. Because they had the cubes to use, investigating these numbers was accessible to all of the children, even those who were less confident numerically. Also, investigating these numbers gave the children experience that could be useful for them when making predictions about which of the smaller numbers are even or odd.

CHAPTER FIFTEEN
ESTIMATING WITH ONE HUNDRED

Overview

This two-day lesson gives children the opportunity to examine collections of different objects and estimate whether there are more or less than one hundred of each. Later, the students count the objects in several different ways. The activity provides children experience with counting, estimating, and the important landmark number of one hundred. The lesson also models for children a way to collect and organize data and gives them practice with addends that total the number of children in the class.

Materials

▲ 1-gallon clear plastic bags with twist tops, 1 per student
▲ collections of objects to fill the bags: cubes, color tiles, pencils, crayons, beans, toothpicks, small plastic animals, small paper clips, large paper clips, pattern blocks, keys, counters, cotton swabs
▲ one paper bag filled with a dozen or so objects

Time

▲ two class periods

Teaching Directions

1. Prepare the plastic bags, one for each student, putting more or less than one hundred of an object in each. Number the bags and secure them with twist ties.

2. Distribute lined paper and ask the children to number their pages from one to the number of children in the class.

3. Talk with the children about what an estimate is. Show them a paper bag and shake it so they can hear that there are objects inside. Talk about the difficulty of estimating when you don't have enough information. Tell the children that with the plastic bags, they can see the objects and, therefore, make reasonable estimates.

4. Explain to the children that they will look at each plastic bag, estimate if there are more or less than one hundred objects in it, and record *more* or *less* next to that bag's number on their papers. Write *more* and *less* on the board. Tell them that they aren't to count all of the objects in order to decide.

5. Distribute the bags, one to each student. After children record, give them a signal to pass each bag to the next child and receive a new one to estimate. Continue in this way until each student has made an estimate for each bag.

6. Next, have each child count the objects in one bag. Talk with them about counting in more than one way, choosing from counting by ones, twos, fives, or tens.

7. To end the period, distribute half sheets of newsprint and ask the students to record what they counted, how they grouped the objects, and any numbers that would help explain what they did.

8. The next day, return the children's papers to them and gather the class for a discussion. Ask each child to report the result and explain how he or she counted. Record the counts on the board by numbering the items as they are in the bags, then labeling two columns *More* and *Less* for the recording counts. As children report, ask the class in which column to record each count.

Object	Actual Count	
	More	Less
1. pencils		72
2. color tiles		85
3. paper clips	179	
4. counters		89
5. keys		92
6. buttons	120	
7. pattern blocks	131	
8. cotton swabs	145	

9. Label two more columns on the board for the children's estimates, one to record how many estimated more than one hundred for each bag, and the other for how many estimated less than one hundred. After having children raise their hands for both columns for several of the items, ask for hands only if they estimated more. Then ask children to use that information to figure out how many estimated less.

Object	Actual Count		Estimates	
	More	Less	More	Less
1. pencils		72	2	15
2. color tiles		85		
3. paper clips	179			
4. counters		89		
5. keys		92		
6. buttons	120			
7. pattern blocks	131			
8. cotton swabs	145			

10. Finally, ask children to examine the data you recorded. Lead a class discussion for them to talk about what they notice.

Teaching Notes

The number one hundred is a landmark number in our number system. When we begin counting the days we are in school at the beginning of the year, children can't picture how far into the future it will be when we finally get to the hundredth day. One hundred seems like a huge number to first graders, some of whom can't yet count that high. Children need many experiences with one hundred. They benefit from thinking about the relative magnitude of the number—that it's a huge number if you are talking about elephants but a very small number if you are counting grains of rice.

This lesson has several other benefits. When children count the objects to verify their estimates, they do so in several ways—by ones, twos, fives, and tens. Later, they have practice with adding and subtracting when they use the number of children who estimated more for each object to figure out how many children estimated less.

The Lesson

▲▲▲

DAY 1

To prepare for this lesson, I filled 1-gallon plastic bags with collections of objects, choosing items from the classroom with which students were familiar. I filled one bag for each of the seventeen students and numbered the bags from 1 to 17. I used objects of varying sizes—cubes, color tiles, pencils, crayons, beans, toothpicks, small plastic animals, small paper clips, large paper clips, pattern blocks, keys, counters, and cotton swabs. I also put about a dozen cubes in a brown paper bag.

While I didn't count the items, I made sure that some of the plastic bags contained more than one hundred and some contained less. This required me to do some estimating of my own. I found myself counting out groups of ten and then using the groups as visual benchmarks to decide on how many items to put in a bag. I found this more difficult with small objects, like beans,

than with things like pencils. I made a mental note to watch how my students dealt with these same issues. I also made sure that I had roughly the same number of bags with more than one hundred objects and less than one hundred.

To begin the lesson I gave each child a piece of lined paper and asked them to number their papers from 1 to 17 because there were seventeen children in the class and each child would begin with one bag. I gave further directions before I distributed the bags. "I've made collections of things from around the room and put them in these plastic bags," I told them. "You'll have a chance to look at each bag and make an estimate about how many are inside it. Who remembers what an estimate is?" Several children raised their hands. I called on Jaleesa.

"It's sort of like a guess," she said.

I responded, "It is a bit like a guess. An estimate is like a smart guess. It's a guess where you already know something about the thing you're guessing about."

I showed them a brown paper bag and shook it so they could hear that there was something inside. "What if I asked you to guess how many things are in this bag?"

"But what's in the bag?" Gita asked.

"That's a good question," I answered. "If you knew what kind of thing was in the bag and how big it was, it might be easier to guess how many there are. But you still couldn't see them, so it would be hard to tell. If I wanted you to estimate how many there are, I'd let you know what was inside and let you see one or maybe a few of them. For our activity today, you'll be able to see what's inside the bag so you can make your estimate."

I gave one last direction before distributing the plastic bags. "Don't count all of the items in the bag. And don't open the bags. Just look to estimate whether you think the bag has more than one hundred items or fewer than one hundred items."

I gave the bag numbered 1 to the child closest to me and moved around the room, giving the rest out in order. The children were eager to see the contents of the bags and fingered them through the clear plastic.

As I distributed the bags, I said, "Look and think about whether the bag has more than a hundred or less than a hundred things in it. Remember that this is just an estimate—your best guess about whether there are more or fewer than one hundred items in the bag. We'll check later."

After a minute, I asked for the children's attention and said, "Find the number written on the bag, and then find that same number on your paper. If you have bag number six, you'll start with number six on your paper. Put your finger on the number on your paper that matches the number on your bag." I gave the children a minute to find both numbers and put their fingers on their papers.

"If you think your bag contains less than one hundred things, write the word *less* next to the number that matches the number on your bag. If you think your bag has more than one hundred objects, write the word *more* next to that number." I wrote *less* and *more* on the board as I gave these directions. "I'll give you another minute to examine your bag and decide and then write on your paper."

When I noticed that everyone had recorded, I called the class to attention again. I said, "Now you'll each pass your bag to the person next to you. Then do the same for your new bag. Look at it, then find the matching number on your paper and write *more* or *less* to show if you think your bag has more or less than one hundred objects." I explained my plan for passing the bags again so that every student would know whom to pass his or her bag to each time.

I gave the class about a minute to a minute and a half to look at each bag and record. When I noticed that most of the children had written their predictions, I told the children to pass their bags to the next person, encouraging those who were slower to hurry and record.

The children were eager and excited. They looked carefully at each bag and considered its contents. I noticed they gave some bags more careful thought than others. I asked Sammye about this as I watched her scrutinize a bag of crayons.

"I see that you're spending more time looking at this bag of crayons than you did the bag of beans. When you had the bag of beans, you wrote your estimate down almost immediately. Was that one easier than the bag of crayons in some way?"

She answered, "No, the beans were hard. I couldn't count them all because they were all rolling around together. There were a bunch of them, so I just wrote *more*."

Estimating with One Hundred 115

"So how are the crayons different?" I continued.

Sammye said, "See, here are ten of them." I could see she had separated ten crayons from the others with her fingers. "This is ten, but I don't think there's nine more tens in the bag, so I'm going to write *less*." Sammye was a bright girl who loved math. She was very verbal and was growing in her ability to describe her mathematical thinking.

When I asked Travis the same question about the bag of beans, he shrugged and said, "I think there's a lot of beans in here." He had written *more* for the bean bag and *more* for the crayon bag as well. He hadn't manipulated the crayons inside the bag but had written down his guess after merely looking.

Ann was obviously counting the beans in the bag. When I asked her to tell me about what she was doing to decide, Ann said, "I'm counting as far as I can get. Then when you tell us to pass them, I think about whether to write *more* or *less*." Ann came to my classroom speaking no English, but her number sense was terrific. I knew that Ann was using the information she was gathering with the quick counts to make her predictions.

When each child had recorded for all of the bags, I said, "Now we're going to find out how many each bag really contains. You are going to open the bag you now have at your desk and count the contents in two ways. What are some ways you could count?"

Sergio spoke up. "By ones," he said.

Other children called out this suggestions: "By twos." "By fives." "By tens."

I said, "Yes, you can count by ones, twos, fives, or tens. When you have finished counting the second time, leave the objects as you grouped them on your desk so we can talk about them." I asked each student

to record the number he or she counted next to the estimate on his or her paper for that bag number.

The children emptied the bags and began counting. Many of them started counting by ones. About half the students arranged their objects on their desks in groups of twos, fives, or tens. (See Figures 15–1 through 15–5.)

While the children were counting, I walked around the room observing the way they grouped their objects. I stopped at Jamie's desk. "How did you count your color tiles?" I asked.

"I made stacks of five," he answered. "I have nine stacks and four left over. That makes forty-nine. I was right because I guessed there were less than one hundred."

Ann said, "I put mine in twos to count." She had the cotton swabs lined up in groups of two across her desk.

"What is your total?" I asked.

"I got seventy-two," she answered.

Togo had counted small paper clips. "I made piles of ten. So I just counted ten, twenty, thirty, forty, fifty, sixty, seventy, eighty, ninety. I almost had a hundred, but I only counted four more."

Next I distributed a half sheet of newsprint to each child and said, "Record on this paper what you've done today. I'm interested in having a record of your counting experience. Write about what you counted, how you grouped your objects, and any numbers that would help us understand your work. This will allow us to talk about the counting, even after we put the objects away." The children worked on their recording for the rest of the period, and I collected their papers when they were done.

DAY 2

I began class the next day by returning the children's papers to them, both the ones on

▲▲▲▲▲▲Figure 15–1 *Lori counted trains of five interlocking cubes. She recorded her total as 1,025, then 125, but her recording showed 85 cubes.*

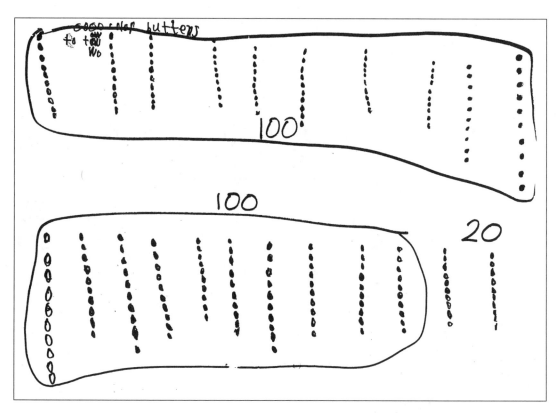

▲▲▲▲▲▲Figure 15–2 *Sanjay counted 120 buttons. He used dots to represent each button and grouped them in tens and hundreds.*

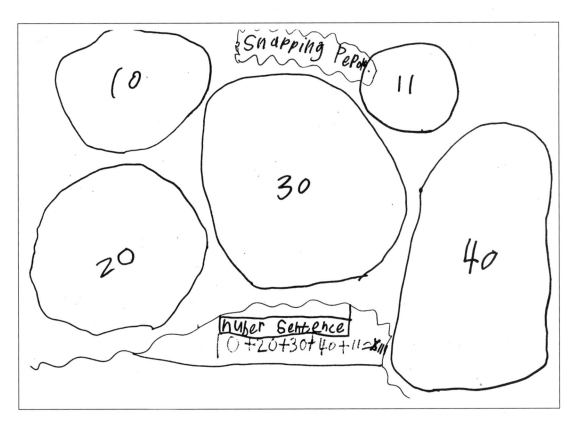

▲▲▲▲▲▲Figure 15–3 *Kurt put his plastic snapping people in piles, with each pile having more than the last. He had 11 plastic people left and wrote a number sentence to show that he was combining the amounts.*

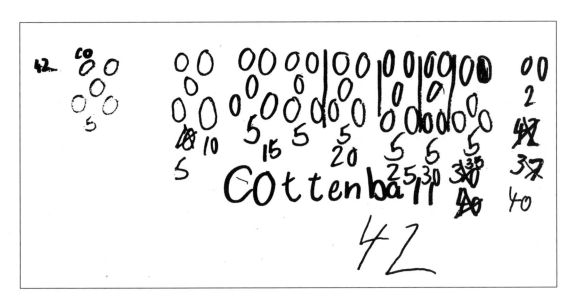

▲▲▲▲▲▲Figure 15–4 *Ace skipped a group of five when he counted, giving him a total of 37. He recounted to get his final total of 42.*

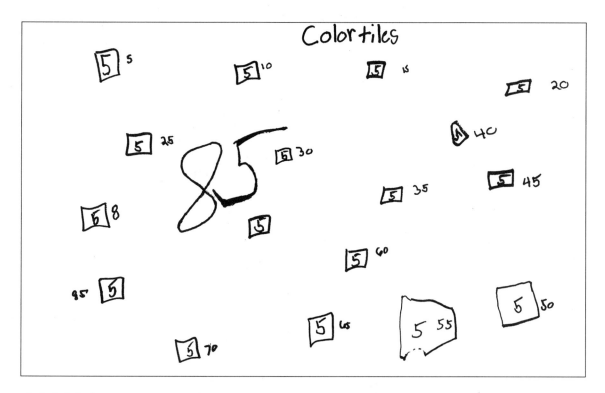

▲▲▲▲▲▲**Figure 15–5** *Terezia put her color tiles in stacks of five, then recorded the running total as she counted by fives.*

which they had recorded their estimates and the newsprint on which they had explained their counts. I gathered the class on the rug near the front of the room. One by one, the children explained to the class how they had counted. As each child shared his or her final result, the other children checked their papers to see what they had predicted for that bag. I heard many exclamations of delight as students learned that their predictions were correct. (See Figure 15–6 on page 120.)

As the children reported, I kept a record of the counts on the board. I listed the objects as I had numbered them in the bags and recorded the actual count either in the column I had labeled *More* if there were more than one hundred or in a column labeled *Less* if there were fewer than one hundred. When a child reported, I asked the

class in which column I should record the number.

Object	Actual Count	
	More	Less
1. pencils		72
2. color tiles		85
3. paper clips	179	
4. counters		89
5. keys		92
6. buttons	120	
7. pattern blocks	131	
8. cotton swabs	145	

When we had recorded the count for each object, I went through the list and asked children to report if they had estimated more for each item. Then we figured out how many had estimated less for each item. This was a way to give the children numerical practice with separating seventeen into two groups.

▲▲▲▲▲▲**Figure 15–6** *After numbering her paper to 17, Crystal circled the number of the bag she started with. Then, as she counted each bag, she circled the number to keep track of where she was. The checks showed which of her predictions were correct.*

I began this part of the activity by saying, "Find number one on your list again and raise your hand if you estimated there were more than one hundred pencils." Two hands went up.

I then asked, "How many of you predicted less than one hundred?" I counted fifteen hands.

I ruled two more columns on the board to record the number of children who estimated more and less and recorded the 2 and the 15 in the correct places.

Object	Actual Count		Estimates	
	More	Less	More	Less
1. pencils		72	2	15
2. color tiles		85		
3. paper clips	179			
4. counters		89		
5. keys		92		
6. buttons	120			
7. pattern blocks	131			
8. cotton swabs	145			

"Let's see," I wondered out loud. "Did everyone raise a hand? Let's see if I counted seventeen hands. I'll add fifteen plus two. That's fifteen . . . sixteen, seventeen. Yes, it's seventeen, so I've got everyone."

I continued in this way for two more items, recording the number of children who had estimated more and who had estimated less and checking that they added up to seventeen each time.

Object	Actual Count		Estimates	
	More	Less	More	Less
1. pencils		72	2	15
2. color tiles		85	8	
3. paper clips	179		14	3
4. counters		89		
5. keys		92		
6. buttons	120			
7. pattern blocks	131			
8. cotton swabs	145			

When I got to the bag that contained counters, I took the count for the number of children who had estimated more. There were six. I recorded this on the chart and said to the class, "I think that we can use the information that six children estimated more to figure out how many children estimated less. Who has an idea about how we can do that?"

Jaleesa suggested, "You can minus that from seventeen."

"Can you tell us how that would work, Jaleesa?" I asked.

"Well, if you look at the pencils on the chart, there were two people who guessed more than a hundred and all the rest guessed less. So if you take two away from seventeen you get fifteen, and that's how many people raised their hands for less than a hundred."

"Or you could count," Ricky said.

"How would you count?" I asked.

"I'd go six . . . ," Ricky said, and then started holding up fingers as he counted, "seven, eight, nine . . ." He continued to seventeen. "It's eleven," he said.

"So you think that eleven children estimated less," I said, connecting Ricky's counting to the context of estimates.

"That's right," Sammye said. "I subtracted like Jaleesa said. It's eleven."

"Is there any other way we could figure out how many children estimated less?" I asked.

"We could raise our hands," Serena said.

"Yes, that's a good way to check," I said. "Look at your papers again and find item number four, counters. If you estimated less than one hundred for counters, raise your hand." I counted to verify that eleven was correct.

For the rest of the items, I took the count for how many had estimated more and we used Jaleesa's and Ricky's strategies to figure out how many had estimated less.

When the chart was made, I asked the children what they noticed about the data on it. "Talk with your neighbor about what you notice," I said. "Then you'll have a chance to share your ideas with the rest of the class."

The children talked to one another for a few minutes, pointing to the chart as they did. As they talked, I walked around the room listening in on snatches of conversations. I think listening to individual discussions helps me structure a balanced class discussion. Sometimes I'm able to encourage a student to share an idea that I think would benefit others. Other times I'm able to hear differences of opinion and ask the children to discuss their ideas.

After a few minutes, I called the class to attention and asked for pairs of students to report about their discussions. Togo and Gita spoke right up. "We think the tall things were easier to guess," Gita said.

"What do you mean by 'tall things'?" I asked.

Togo answered, "Like the pencils and the cotton swabs. We mostly guessed those right."

"Does anyone have an idea about why those might have been easier to predict?" I asked.

"I could line them all up and see how many there were," Jamie said.

Jaleesa added, "I couldn't really count them all before you made us pass them, but I could count some of them, so I knew there weren't a hundred pencils."

"I made tens because they were easy to hold from the outside of the bag. I thought there was less than one hundred, too," Gita said.

I then asked, "Who has another observation about the chart?"

Ricky responded, "The little things were the hardest to guess." He came up to the chart and pointed to the data for paper clips, two-color counters, and buttons. "Some of us thought more, some of us thought less. I just guessed. I couldn't count them like the pencils."

De'Witt said, "I just looked and guessed."

It was time to end the period, so I collected the children's papers and had them get ready for recess.

Questions and Discussion

▲▲

▲ *Aren't students sometimes tempted to change their estimates to match the results in order to be "right"?*

Some children are highly invested in being right, especially if that is what they have seen valued in their classrooms. Children should feel the freedom to make mistakes in math, to see mistakes not as calamities, but as opportunities to learn. To encourage this, it's important to accept all kinds of estimates, even when your goal is for students to make reasonable estimates. This kind of lesson, which requires that students think only about whether there are more or less than one hundred, allows students to practice estimating in an easier way than coming up with a particular number. The more opportunities children have to make and use estimates, the better they become at estimating and the less likely they are to feel intimidated by doing so.

▲ *I think that some children would be able to analyze the chart easily while others wouldn't have a clue where to begin. How do you handle this?*

I know that there will be a wide range of responses to an open-ended question like the one I posed. Some children will look at the chart and see trends and make generalizations while others may just be thinking about what the numbers on the chart represent. I don't worry if all students aren't able to participate in our discussion at the same level. I think it's important to expose all the children in my class to conversations that may expand their mathematical thinking. I never know when something said in a class discussion will spark new understanding for one or more students.

CHAPTER SIXTEEN
THE HUNDREDS CHART

Overview

The hundreds chart is a valuable instructional tool for emphasizing the patterns inherent in our base ten system. Examining the positions of the numbers on the hundreds chart and the patterns in the arrangement helps children think about the magnitudes of the numbers, compute mentally, learn to count on, and become fluent in thinking about what is ten more or ten less than any number less than one hundred. This lesson includes five different learning activities using the hundreds chart: *Learning About the Hundreds Chart, Skip-Counting, Looking for Patterns, Developing Computational Strategies,* and *Solving Story Problems.* The activities are presented in the order in which they should be introduced; each can be repeated throughout the year to reinforce and extend children's learning.

Materials

▲ 1–100 pocket wall chart, with number cards that can be removed
▲ squares of transparent colored paper, the same size as the number cards, about 50 of one color
▲ 1–100 charts, 1 per student (see Blackline Masters)

Time

▲ twenty to thirty minutes, repeated throughout the year

Teaching Directions

Learning About the Hundreds Chart

1. Post a hundreds pocket chart with all the numbers inserted. After it has been visible in the classroom for a while, remove about half of the number cards, leaving the numbers from 1 to 12 and an assortment of others.

2. Hold up the number 13 and ask for a volunteer to place it where it belongs on the chart. Have the child explain his or her reasoning. Continue with other numbers.

3. When the children's attention for placing numbers wanes, stop the activity and continue over the next few days until the chart is complete.

4. At other times during the year, again remove cards and ask children to place them where they belong. Vary the cards you remove, either removing the cards from one section of the chart, from one or two rows or columns, or in some other pattern.

Skip-Counting

1. Ask the children to count aloud by fives, each saying one number in the sequence and remembering it. Suggest that they each write down their number if they think they might forget it.

2. Ask children, one by one, to come up to the hundreds chart and place a transparent colored square over their numbers. Do not attempt to have them place numbers in order; rather, choose children so that the order is random.

3. When about ten children have placed colored transparent squares, ask the children if they can predict where the next square might go. Let all who have an idea share their thinking.

4. Then continue having children place their numbers until all of the multiples of five have been highlighted.

5. Leave the colored transparent squares on the chart for several more days to give the class time to look at the pattern.

6. Repeat the activity during the year for skip-counting by twos, threes, fours, tens, and twenties.

Looking for Patterns

1. Distribute a hundreds chart to each pair of students and instruct them to look for patterns and be ready to share what they've found with the class.

2. After a few minutes, call the class to attention and ask children to share what they have discovered. As they report, record their discoveries on a class chart. Continue until all children who want to report have the chance to do so.

Developing Computational Strategies

1. Ask: "How much is ten more than sixty-seven?" Have the class count with you as you move your finger ten spaces after 67 on the hundreds chart and land on 77. Repeat: "How much is ten more than forty-two?" Again, have the class count with you.

2. Tell the children that you're going to close your eyes and touch a number on the chart. The class should tell you the number you touched, and you'll tell them the number that is right below it. Do this for several numbers until the children can explain how you predicted. Then ask for a volunteer to explain what you were doing.

3. Give several students the chance to come up to the chart and, without looking, touch a number. Have the class identify the number and the child predict what number is right below it. Vary the activity by asking the child at the chart to identify the number that is right above the one he or she is touching.

4. Give the children practice counting by tens beginning with different numbers. Say: "Let's start with eight and then say the number that is ten more, then ten more than that, and so on." As the children identify the numbers, list them on the board in a vertical list, ending with ninety-eight. If no one notices, point out that the numbers you listed also appear on the hundreds chart. Then ask: "What number would come next?"

5. Give a hundreds chart to each pair of students. Choose a starting number for the class and have half of the students count by tens aloud together while the other half checks on their charts. Repeat, reversing the roles. Then have students do the same activity in pairs.

Solving Story Problems

1. Write a subtraction problem on the board:

Patrick collected 52 toy cars. He had room for 38 of them on his shelf. How many cars did not fit on his shelf?

2. Ask: "What kind of mathematical action is happening in this story?" Children may identify addition or subtraction, depending on how they think about the problem.

3. Ask children for suggestions about how to solve the problem and for a number sentence that describes the problem. Record their ideas on the board.

4. Show how to use the hundreds chart both to count up from 38 to 52 and to count backward from 52 to 38, using what they learned about counting up and down by tens.

5. Ask students for other problems to solve in this way. Repeat over the next several weeks.

Teaching Notes

In first grade, children begin to count to and recognize numbers greater than twenty. On the first day of school, I hang a hundreds pocket chart with removable numbers and use it for various activities throughout the year. As children's knowledge grows to include large numbers, the hundreds chart provides them with a useful visual model of our number system. The chart helps children explore numerical patterns that they then use to strengthen their number sense and develop expertise with addition and subtraction.

We refer to the hundreds chart often in class. Students glance at the chart when they want to write a number but don't remember what it looks like. Sometimes they use it to determine whether a number is more or less than another number when playing a game. Also, many children develop strategies for addition and subtraction that make use of the hundreds chart.

The Lesson

▲▲

LEARNING ABOUT THE HUNDREDS CHART

The hundreds chart had been posted in my room since the first day of school. About a month after school had started, one morning before the children arrived, I moved the chart down to a height within reach for the children and removed just over half of the number cards. I left on the chart the numbers from 1 to 12 and then about thirty others, leaving random gaps.

I began the lesson by holding up the number 13 and asking, "Who knows where this number belongs?"

"That's easy!" Jesse exclaimed. "Right next to the twelve!" There were nods and words of agreement around the room.

"What about this number?" I continued, holding up the 19. "Raise your hand if you think you know where it belongs." I waited until many hands were up and then called on Kiki. She came up to the front of the room, took the card, and correctly located it on the chart just before the 20.

I asked, "Why did you put it there?"

Kiki answered, "When you count, you say nineteen, then twenty. So it has to go before the twenty."

I continued with several other of the missing numbers, each time asking the child who placed the number to explain his or her reasoning. When I noticed the children's interest waning, I stopped for the day, went on with the other part of the lesson I had planned, and resumed the activity the next day. It took three days to replace all of the cards I had removed.

This is an activity that students benefit from doing several times in the year. Every month or so, I repeated it with different assortments of number cards missing from the chart. Sometimes I removed the cards from one section of the chart, perhaps somewhere in the middle. Sometimes I removed one or two complete rows or columns. The variety keeps the children interested and encourages them to use the patterns on the chart in different ways to place missing numbers. This activity is particularly useful for students who become dependent on beginning to count with one, even when the numbers being used are relatively far away from one.

SKIP-COUNTING

The chart is also useful for visually interpreting skip-counting. I introduce this activity after students are familiar with the sequence of counting by fives. I use a hundreds chart with all number cards inserted in the pockets and transparent colored squares of paper the same size as the number cards so that they also fit into the pockets. The transparent squares are effective for highlighting specific numbers on the chart.

I said to the class one day, "Today we're going to practice counting by fives again. I'll point to you when it's your turn to say the next number in the sequence." This was a familiar activity in the class that we did in spare moments such as when we were lined up and waiting to go to the library or the auditorium, when we gathered back in the classroom after recess, and so on.

On this day, I gave a new direction. I said, "This time, be sure to remember your number after you say it. If you think you might forget the number you said, jot it down on a piece of paper." I waited a couple of minutes while some students took out paper and pencils.

I then said, "Ready? Here we go!" I began pointing to students, slowly so everyone could keep up with the pattern of skip-counting by fives. When all twenty-four children had said a number, we had reached 120.

"Now here's the new part," I said. "I'm going to call out each person's name, and when I do, I want you to come to the hundreds chart, take a yellow transparent square, and place it over your number to highlight it on the chart. Then we'll look at the pattern of yellow squares. Mickey, will you start us off?"

Mickey came to the front of the room where the hundreds chart was hanging within his reach. He checked the little slip of paper he carried and placed a transparent square over the number 25. Next I called on Pete. He placed his square over the number 60. I continued to call students up to highlight their numbers. Because I didn't call them up in the same order I had called on them to say their numbers, the pattern on the chart built randomly.

After ten children had highlighted their numbers, I said, "Kiki will go next. But before Kiki highlights her number, can anyone describe where it might go?"

Christopher raised his hand. He said, "I think it will go in the fives column or in the tens column, because that's where all the others are."

Chanell added, "That's because when you count by fives, you always say numbers like twenty-five, thirty-five, forty-five, but you never say twenty-four or forty-seven or anything like that."

"Does anyone else have an idea to share?" I asked.

Rick raised his hand. "If you add five plus five you get ten, and all the numbers under ten are yellow. Or they will be yellow."

Kiki came up and correctly highlighted her number, 50. I continued calling on children to highlight their numbers until all the multiples of five were yellow.

"What about us?" Alisa cried. She was one of the four children who had numbers greater than one hundred and couldn't place their yellow squares on the chart.

"Hmm, we'll have to extend the chart for your numbers to fit," I said. "Since the chart is on the chalkboard and there is space below, why don't you write your number where you think it belongs." Alisa's number was 105. She took a piece of yellow chalk and wrote it in under 95. The other three children wrote theirs as well.

I didn't remove the yellow squares on the chart for several days, giving the children more time to look at the pattern. A week or so later we repeated the activity, this time skip-counting by threes. During the year, we did the same activity for tens, twos, fours, and twenties.

LOOKING FOR PATTERNS

Looking for patterns on the hundreds chart helps students understand the structure of our number system. For this activity, I distributed a copy of the hundreds chart to each pair of children so that they could more closely examine the placement of numbers.

I instructed the class, "With your partner, look at the chart and see what patterns you can discover. Be ready to share a pattern with the class." As students talked, I walked around the room listening in on their discussions. Sometimes I stopped and asked a question and sometimes I just listened, taking mental notes about conversations I could use for a whole-class discussion.

Fouzia and Ann were talking about the pattern of even numbers on the chart. Fouzia said, "Look! Two, four, six, eight, ten."

"Here's another two," Ann said, pointing to the 2 in the number 12.

"And here's four, six, eight again!" Fouzia said. "And look here under the ten, all the numbers have a zero in them."

Fouzia and Ann were moving quickly from one discovery to another. I didn't want to stop the flow of their thinking by asking a question. However, I made a mental note to talk to the class later about the pattern of even and odd numbers on the chart.

Jonathan and De'Witt were both silent when I walked by their desks. "What have you noticed so far?" I asked.

De'Witt scratched his head and said, "There sure are a lot of numbers on this chart."

"How many numbers do you think there are on the chart?" I asked.

"Maybe a hundred?" Jonathan answered without much conviction.

"How could you find out for sure?" I asked.

De'Witt started to count right away. Jonathan watched him and when De'Witt got to thirty, Jonathan observed, "You don't have to count all those numbers, you can just count by tens. See, ten, twenty, thirty . . ." De'Witt joined in and the boys counted by tens to one hundred.

After about five minutes, I asked for the children's attention. "Who would like to share a pattern you noticed on the chart?" I asked. Many children were eager to share. I called on Jesse and Rick first.

"We saw that all the numbers in the last column have a zero," Jesse said.

Rick added, "They are like count-by-tens numbers—ten, twenty, thirty, forty . . ." The rest of the class joined in as Rick counted aloud.

"We found that, too!" Kiana exclaimed. More heads nodded as children recognized that pattern.

I recorded Jesse and Rick's idea on a large piece of chart paper:

All the numbers in the last column have a zero. You can count them by 10s.

I called on Lori next. She and Alisa were wiggling excitedly about a discovery they had made. They came to the front of the room to point out their pattern on the large hundreds chart. Lori put her finger on the number 1 in the upper left corner. She then moved her finger diagonally down to the bottom right corner.

She said, "See, here's the one, and then here's a one and a two, then a two and a three."

Alisa chimed in, "It's twelve, then twenty-three, then thirty-four. Like, the second number is always first in the next box."

Lori spoke again. "It goes like that all the way down until you get to the one hundred."

I recorded the girls' pattern on the chart paper:

The second digit in each box on the diagonal is the first digit in the next box.

Even though neither Lori nor Alisa had used the words *diagonal* and *digit*, I incorporated them into what I recorded. Then I read to the class what I had written. I find that the best way to teach new terminology is to use it in the context of an activity.

This pattern was hard for some students to see. I estimated that about half the students in the class really understood what Lori and Alisa had explained, but I didn't belabor the point. Many other students were waiting to share and I knew we could return to this pattern later.

I asked for more volunteers, and Sanjay and Mickey came up next. "We found that all the numbers under the number four have a four in them and all the numbers under the five have a five in them," Sanjay said. Mickey pointed to illustrate what Sanjay had explained. The rest of the students looked at their charts. Some noticed that other columns had a similar pattern. As they noticed this they began talking all at once, showing their charts to one another and pointing to the other columns. As the children talked among themselves, I recorded on the chart:

All of the numbers under the four have a four in them; all of the numbers under the five have a five in them; the same is true for the other numbers.

Christopher then spoke out. "It works for the rows going the other way, too. But they're all fifties."

"What do you mean, Christopher?" I asked.

"In the up-and-down rows, the five is always five. Like, thirty-five, forty-five, fifty-five, sixty-five. But the other way it's always fifty: fifty-one, fifty-two, fifty-three, fifty-four . . ."

"What does the five mean in the number thirty-five?" I asked.

"That means just five. But the fives going across mean fifty," Christopher said. Christopher's explanation revealed his understanding of place value. However, I knew that many children in the class didn't understand Christopher's insight. Place value relies on a complex set of concepts, and it takes many experiences for children to develop understanding.

After calling for the students' attention, I asked for other patterns they had noticed. Melony and Kiki raised their hands excitedly. "All of the numbers with two of the same number are in a slanting line," Melony said.

"Show us what you mean," I requested. The girls came to the hundreds chart and pointed to the 11, then to the 22, the 33, the 44, and so on, down to the 99.

"So all of these numbers in this diagonal line have the same digit in the ones and tens places?" I asked, again using the words *diagonal* and *digit*.

"Yes," Kiki answered. I recorded:

Starting with 11, the numbers in the diagonal have the same digit in the ones and tens places.

English was the second language for both of these girls. Verbalizing their mathematical understanding helped them become more fluent. I try to establish an atmosphere in the classroom in which we accept one another's ideas and contribute by adding to them. I encourage students to express mathematical ideas and use correct sentence structure, and I help them develop their vocabularies.

I continued having students share the patterns they noticed so that everyone who wanted had a chance to report.

DEVELOPING COMPUTATIONAL STRATEGIES

Once children become comfortable with the format of the hundreds chart, they can use the chart as a tool for helping them add and subtract numbers less than one hundred. Typically each year, several children notice that they can use the hundreds chart to help them count on. Their discovery can spark a discussion that leads to investigating more sophisticated addition and subtraction strategies. However, if no child makes this observation, I bring it up after we've talked about patterns and initiate a discussion.

"How much is ten more than sixty-seven?" I asked the children one day, putting my finger on the 67 on the hundreds chart. "Let's use the hundreds chart to count." The class counted out loud as I moved my finger. I stopped when we had counted ten numbers and landed on the 77.

I repeated the question with another number. "How much is ten more than forty-two?" Again, I put my finger on the 42 and the children counted ten more with me to the 52.

Then I said, "This time I'm going to close my eyes and touch a number on the chart. You will tell me the number I'm pointing to, and I'll tell you the number that's right below it on the chart. Then you can let me know if I'm right. Let's try it." I closed my eyes and touched a space on the chart.

"Fifty-seven!" they called out in unison.

"Sixty-seven," I said quickly.

I touched another number. "Eighty-two!" they exclaimed.

"Ninety-two," I responded.

I touched one more number. "Sixteen!" the class said.

"Twenty-six," I answered.

"Let me try!" several children called out.

"Who thinks you know how to do what I did?" I asked.

Several children raised their hands and I called on Lori. She came up to the chart, closed her eyes, and pointed to a number. The class said, "Thirty-three."

Lori reacted quickly. "Forty-three," she said.

"How did you do that, Lori?" I asked.

"It's easy," she answered. "It's always ten more. If you go down one box, it's like ten more."

Lori took another turn, and then I called on two other students to come up, close their eyes, and choose numbers. Each time the class called out the number the student was touching, and each time the student called out the number that was ten more. Although Lori had correctly explained the pattern, and the other two children were successful, I knew that some students would need further experiences to understand and apply the pattern.

I continued, next calling on Kiana to come to the front of the room. I began by giving her the same instructions I had given the other students. "Close your eyes and touch a spot on the chart."

The class called out, "Sixty-two."

"This time I want you to tell me which number is above the number you touched," I said.

"That's easy!" Kiana exclaimed. "It's just opposite of what Lori said."

"What do you mean, Kiana?" I asked.

She answered, "It has to be . . . um . . . fifty-two. When you go down, the number is ten bigger, so when you go up, the number has to be ten littler."

I directed Kiana again to put her finger on a number, and this time I instructed her to identify the number just below it. She did so correctly. I followed this by having two more students demonstrate naming the numbers on the chart that were above and below the number they touched.

Then, to be sure that all the students would have an opportunity to work with these patterns, I shifted the lesson from a whole-class activity to one the children would do in pairs. I distributed copies of the hundreds chart, one to each pair of students. I explained, "Now you'll have the chance to try using this pattern to identify numbers on the hundreds chart. You and your partner will take turns closing your eyes and touching a number on the chart. Your partner will tell you what number you are touching and then ask you to name the number either above or below the one you are touching. Then you'll switch roles and play again." As students worked, I could hear them becoming more confident in their ability to quickly identify the numbers that were ten more or ten less than the numbers they touched.

The next day I began a new activity to support students' thinking about this same context. "Today we're going to count by tens, starting with a number, then saying the number that is ten more, then ten more than that, and so on," I began.

"That's easy," Kiki said. She started to count out loud, "Ten, twenty, thirty, ..."

I interrupted Kiki before she got to one hundred and said, "That's the idea, but this time we're not going to start with ten. Let's try starting with eight."

"You can't start with eight and count by tens!" Alisa announced.

"Are you sure, Alisa?" I asked. "What's ten more than eight?"

Alisa thought for a moment. "Eighteen," she replied.

"And ten more than eighteen?" I asked.

I noticed many children counting on their fingers. They returned to this familiar way of adding by counting whenever they faced a new challenge. Although they had worked with the hundreds chart just the day before, they weren't comfortable enough with it yet to use it to solve a new problem.

After counting on her fingers, Alisa said, "Twenty-eight." On the board I wrote 8, 18, and 28 vertically, they way they would appear on a hundreds chart:

8
18
28

Kurt began to wave his hand wildly. "I know what comes next," he said excitedly. "Thirty-eight! The tens numbers are going one, two, three, four. Then comes forty-eight." I recorded *38* and *48*, and the class picked up the pattern, chanting together, "Fifty-eight, sixty-eight, seventy-eight,

eighty-eight, ninety-eight." I recorded as they called out the numbers.

We heard one small voice continue the pattern, "Tenty-eight." The class broke out in giggles.

"That's how the pattern goes," I said, and then added, "but that's not how we say the number that's ten more than ninety-eight. What number should we say?"

"One hundred eight!" several children shouted. I reminded them to be polite to the class next door by keeping their voices down.

"Does this column of numbers look familiar to you?" I then asked the class.

Chanell broke into a big smile. "I know! It's the chart from yesterday."

I responded, "You're right, Chanell, it's a piece of that chart. Today you'll check yourselves as we count by tens starting with different numbers." I handed out a chart to each student.

I then explained, "Let's begin by turning the charts facedown on your desks, and I'll clip this poster on top of the big hundreds chart so we can't see it. We'll start with thirty-six, we'll count by tens, and then check ourselves with the hundreds chart. We'll go slowly so that everyone has a chance to think before we say the next number. But in order to check ourselves, I'm going to divide the class in half so that half of you are counting out loud and half of you are following along on your hundreds charts. That way, if anyone gets stuck, you'll have the other half of the class to help you get unstuck."

Using my arm to motion, I said, "OK, this half of the class will be the counters the first time, and this half will be the checkers. Let's start with thirty-six."

The counting students counted together, "Thirty-six, forty-six, fifty-six, sixty-six, seventy-six, eighty-six, ninety-six," while the others followed along on their papers, nodding. Then I reversed the roles, this time choosing twenty-seven as the starting number. I repeated this several times, choosing a different starting number each time.

Once I was sure all of the children understood the system, I turned this into a partner activity so students could practice individually and partners could check each other. In the whole group, individual voices are easily lost in the crowd. However, when students work in pairs, I'm able to circulate and find out if someone is having difficulty. The next day we continued the partner activity, this time counting backward by ten each time.

SOLVING STORY PROBLEMS

Several days later, I presented a problem to the children to give them experience using the hundreds chart to solve story problems. I wrote the problem on the board, reading aloud as I did so:

Patrick collected 52 toy cars. He had room for 38 of them on his shelf. How many cars would not fit on his shelf?

"What kind of mathematical action is happening in this story?" I asked.

Antoine raised his hand. "I think it's like subtracting," he said.

"Tell us why you think that, Antoine," I said.

"Well, it's like he has some cars, and he takes some away and puts them on the shelf, and we have to find out how many are left not on the shelf," he explained. I saw heads around the room nodding in agreement.

"How could we figure out how many cars Patrick has that won't fit on his shelf?" I asked.

"We could draw a picture," Melony suggested.

"Any other ideas?" I asked.

"We could write a number sentence," Mickey offered.

"What number sentence could we write?" I asked.

Lori answered, "I think it would be fifty-two minus thirty-eight equals box." I recorded on the board:

$52 - 38 = \square$

Christopher raised his hand tentatively. "I think we could add, too," he said.

"Explain your idea," I said.

Christopher said, "Well, if we add the cars on the shelf and the cars that don't fit, that should equal to fifty-two." He gave me a questioning look.

"I agree so far, Christopher," I said. "Could you write that as a number sentence on the board?"

"I think so," he said. He came to the board and wrote:

$38 + \square = 52$

I said, "So we have two ways to write number sentences that represent this problem about Patrick and his cars. Now think about how to solve the problem without counting by ones, either forward or backward. Last week we spent time working with the hundreds chart learning how to count ten forward and backward from any number. Is there any way we could use that experience to help us solve this problem?"

The class was quiet. After a moment Rick raised his hand and said, pointing to the hundreds chart on the wall as he spoke. "We could take away the tens from fifty-two to forty-two to thirty-two. Then we'd just have to go back eight, you know, like subtracting."

"Let's try that," I suggested. "You got to thirty-two so now we have eight more to subtract."

Rick came up to the chart, put his finger on 32 and began to count backward. He moved his finger as he said each number and used the fingers on his other hand to keep track of how many times he moved. "Thirty-one, thirty, twenty-nine, twenty-eight. That's four more, so it's fourteen."

"What's fourteen?" I asked to bring the attention back to the problem we were trying to solve.

"Fourteen didn't fit on the shelf," Rick answered.

Next, I had all of the students use their individual hundreds charts to do the subtraction themselves, as Rick had.

"I know another way to do it," Christopher said. "It's the adding way."

"Tell us about it, Christopher," I said.

"Well, you start with thirty-eight like it says on the board," he said, pointing to the problem on the board. "Then you just count until you get to fifty-two, like this." Christopher came up to the chart, put his finger on thirty-eight, then moved it to forty-eight. "Ten," he said. He then counted by ones, moving his finger to 49, 50, 51, and 52. He said as he did so, "Eleven, twelve, thirteen, fourteen. It takes fourteen more to get from thirty-eight to fifty-two."

"Let's try another one!" Crystal said.

"Does anyone have a story to get us started? Talk to someone near you and see if you can think of a story we could solve," I said.

After a few minutes I called on Kiana and Terezia. Terezia said, "Kiana has six-teen pieces of bubble gum and Terezia has twenty-nine pieces of bubble gum. If they put all their gum together, how much gum will they have?" I had hoped for a story problem requiring subtraction, the way the example had, but I decided not to comment on that.

"OK, let's try it," I said. "Kiana has sixteen pieces of gum and Terezia has twenty-nine pieces of gum. How much gum do they have together? Use your hundreds charts to figure out the answer."

Rodney spoke up. "Is this a plus or a minus?" he asked.

I responded, "Let me ask you a question to help you decide that for yourself, Rodney. If Kiana has some gum and Terezia has some gum and they put it together, will they have more gum or less gum than they started with?"

Without hesitating, he said, "More. Oh, it must be adding!"

"Try that and see if it makes sense," I suggested.

We worked through several student problems this way. Using the hundreds chart became a favorite way for the children to solve addition and subtraction problems. Problems requiring regrouping with the traditional addition and subtraction algorithms became accessible to first graders, and by the end of the year, several children were able to do these kinds of addition and subtraction problems mentally.

Questions and Discussion

▲▲

▲ *Why is it important to record the children's patterns on a class chart?*

By writing on the chart paper, I modeled for the class how to record mathematical ideas in words. Also, once an idea is on paper, it becomes a more permanent part of the classroom. After the lesson, I posted the chart on the wall so students would have other opportunities to read the statements. One such opportunity was when students "read around the room" during literacy center time. Having the chart posted also helps me in my teaching. In general, I find that if something is hanging on the wall, I am more likely to refer to it during discussion.

▲ *What about the children who don't catch on to using the chart to solve the addition and subtraction story problems?*

I don't expect all children to learn in the same way or on the same time schedule. However, I've found from repeating the activity, both as a whole-class activity and in individual work, that children who are at first unsure and reticent eventually learn to make use of the chart. It's wonderful to see their learning grow as they become aware of how the chart can help them think about numbers.

ASSESSMENTS

Overview

The assessments in this section are intended to model for teachers how to learn more about what students understand as they are learning about arithmetic. The assessments provide glimpses into students' developing sense of number concepts and skills and their ability to use numbers when solving problems. In all of the assessments, students are required to think, reason, and communicate their thinking using pictures and words as well as numbers. Sprinkling assessments like these throughout the year helps provide a picture of each child's developing mathematical thinking as well as showing how the whole class is progressing.

The first assessment, *Marbles,* asks students to think about the combinations of ten marbles, some red and some blue. *Even or Odd?* asks students to identify two numbers as even or odd and explain how they know. The *8 + 9* assessment is designed to give the teacher information about the strategies students use when adding. *How Many Fingers Are There in Our Classroom?* assesses students' ability to solve a problem with large numbers. *Number Stories* asks students to write and solve story problems involving numbers less than twenty. *Flowers in a Flat* presents students with a problem-solving situation in which they must figure out the number of flowers in six six-packs. *Lunch Count* models how to use a daily routine for an assessment.

Teaching Notes

Assessment is a continual part of the teaching process. Assessments help teachers make instructional decisions about when and how to introduce concepts, which activities to choose, what kind of practice is appropriate, and which students need more time or more individual instruction.

There are many ways to assess children's learning in the course of daily instruction. Observing students as they are solving problems or working on investigations, both when they work individually and when they work with classmates, gives valuable information. Having conversations with individual children as they are involved with classwork and listening to what children say in whole-class discussions are other useful tools for providing insights into students' thinking. However, it's also useful to use written assessments throughout the year to record student progress. Such assignments can not only reveal individual children's progress but also provide useful evidence about the entire class.

Written assessments are most effective in first grade after the children have had a good deal of experience talking about their ideas, hearing the ideas of others, and doing written work as part of regular class assignments. Establishing and reinforcing general guidelines will help make written work more effective for assessing children's progress. Help children learn that on their papers they are to use numbers, words, and pictures and include as much information and detail as they can to reveal how they are thinking and reasoning.

It's also important to keep in mind that good assessments mirror good instruction. Assessments should ask children to solve the same kind of problems they do in lessons every day. The difference is that students record their own thinking and work on their own, thus turning regular lessons into assessments.

Marbles

PROMPT

I have ten marbles. Some of them are red and some are blue. How many of each color could I have? What are all the possible combinations of colors?

Asking students to start with the total number of marbles and find the possible combinations of two colors requires them to decompose ten into various combinations of two addends. Children's work will typically show a variety of methods for thinking about the problem and recording what they find. Some students approach the problem randomly, not thinking about how combinations relate and listing only one or a few of the possible combinations. Students who notice and make use of patterns generally find more combinations.

This assessment can be repeated during the year by varying it in several ways. For example, if students had difficulty with this assignment, you might ask them to try solving the problem for a smaller number of marbles. If students can handle more of a challenge, increase the number of marbles, or keep the number the same and add a color so that students must find combinations of three addends that equal ten.

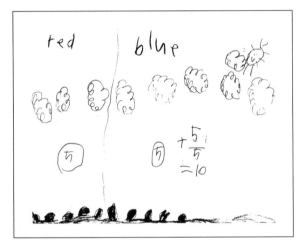

▲▲▲▲▲▲Figure 1 *Nam Thong worked hard to find one combination and record it. She was confused about the correct way to write a number sentence.*

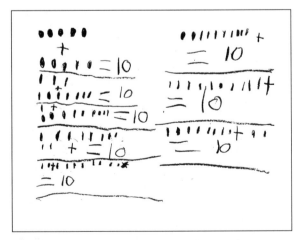

▲▲▲▲▲▲Figure 2 *Santos worked randomly but was able to find eight combinations.*

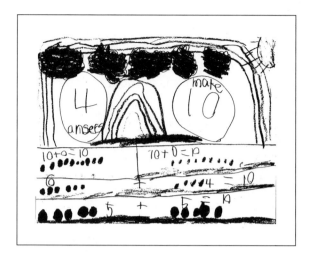

▲▲▲▲▲▲**Figure 3** *Ronnie was pleased with the four combinations he found, even though two were identical.*

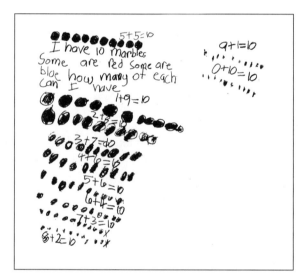

▲▲▲▲▲▲**Figure 4** *After beginning with 5 + 5, Janice was methodical in her recording.*

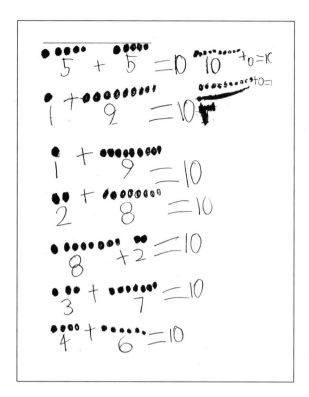

▲▲▲▲▲▲**Figure 5** *Alexa started out with 5 + 5 and then used two colors to show more combinations.*

Even or Odd?

PROMPT

For the numbers 11 and 22, tell whether each is even or odd and explain how you know. You may use any materials in the room that might help you.

Before asking students to do this assessment, make sure they have had many experiences with the concepts of even and odd, thus giving them a variety of classroom experiences to draw upon. It's likely that students will approach the assignment in different ways. In this particular class, some students used tiles or other manipulatives to make pairs; others thought about using the sequence of counting by twos to determine whether a number is even or odd.

▲▲▲▲▲▲**Figure 8** *Caleb used tiles, lining them up to see if each tile would have a partner.*

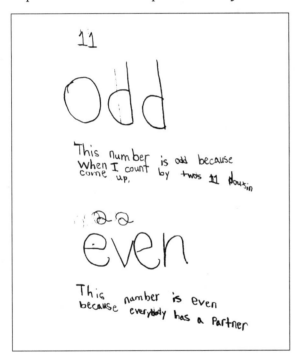

▲▲▲▲▲▲**Figure 6** *Olivia showed even numbers having partners and counting by twos.*

▲▲▲▲▲▲**Figure 9** *Josh also used tiles, but he knew that even numbers can all be counted by twos.*

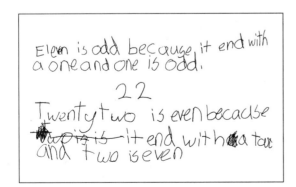

▲▲▲▲▲▲**Figure 7** *Gina thought about using a digit in the ones place.*

8 + 9

PROMPT

Figure out 8 + 9 and write about how you found the answer.

While textbook and worksheet assignments typically ask children to solve a collection of problems like this one, it's useful at times to ask students to focus on one particular problem and explain their reasoning. Repeating this assessment over the year is useful for charting children's progress. Look to see if children are capable of more difficult calculations, if they make the same errors repeatedly, if they are expanding their repertoire of strategies, and so on. At times, you might ask children to find the answer in more than one way.

When observing students working on the problem, keep the following questions in mind:

▲ Does the child choose to use manipulatives?

▲ Does the child draw pictures? Do the pictures accurately represent the process used to solve the problem?

▲ Does the child rearrange quantities to make easier combinations?

▲ Can the child correctly represent the problem symbolically?

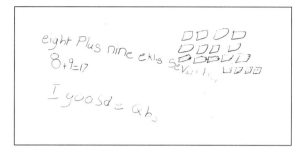

▲▲▲▲▲▲**Figure 11** *Terezia used cubes to solve the problem and recorded with words and numbers.*

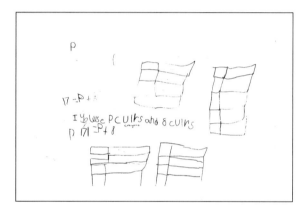

▲▲▲▲▲▲**Figure 12** *Coran wrote:* I used 9 colors and 8 colors. *The representation of the number sentence was still difficult for him.*

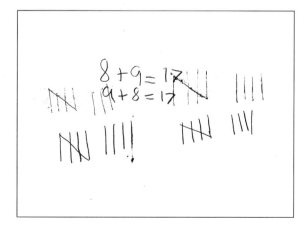

▲▲▲▲▲▲**Figure 13** *Julia showed her understanding of the commutative nature of addition when she reversed the addends in the problem.*

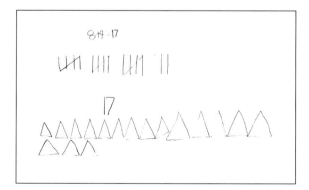

▲▲▲▲▲▲**Figure 10** *Roberto found the answer by counting on his fingers; then he drew pictures to illustrate the answer he found.*

How Many Fingers Are There in Our Classroom?

PROMPT

Figure out how many fingers there are all together on the hands in our classroom.

Figuring out the total number of fingers in the class allows first graders to apply what they know about counting by fives and tens. Also, because the total will usually be close to two hundred, this assessment reveals students' comfort with large numbers. If this problem is too difficult for your students, you might ask them to figure out the number of eyes or thumbs in the class. For a challenge with even larger numbers, ask them to figure out the total number of fingers and toes combined.

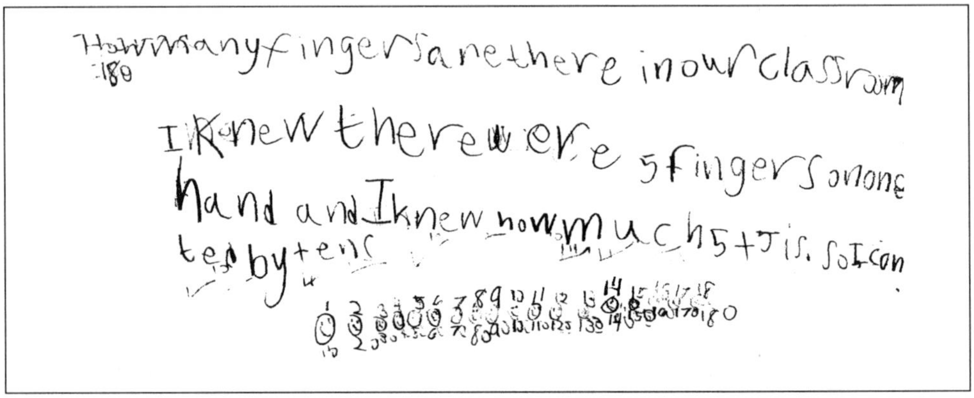

▲▲▲▲▲▲Figure 14   *Ricky thought of 5 + 5 to tell how many fingers each person has, then counted by tens.*

▲▲▲▲▲▲Figure 15   *Lori illustrated her method of counting by fives. Her answer of 190 included the teacher's fingers.*

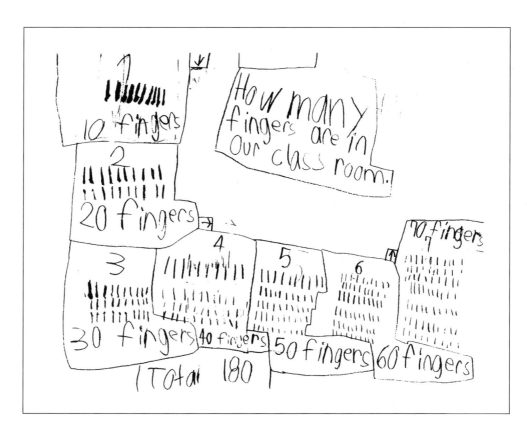

▲▲▲▲▲▲Figure 16 *Jamie began to draw sticks to represent all the fingers one child would have, two children would have, three children would have, and so on, but he abandoned that idea after seven children. He then used the pattern of tens to correctly reach 180 fingers.*

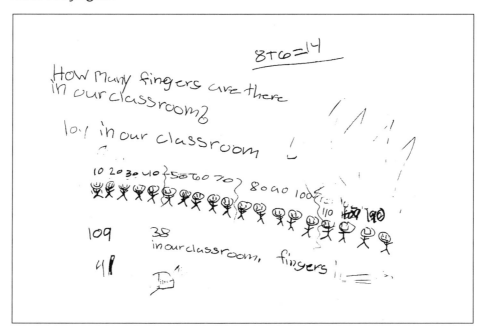

▲▲▲▲▲▲Figure 17 *Kiana drew stick figures to represent the class and began to count the figures by tens; however, she became confused after 100.*

Number Stories

PROMPT

Imagine being on a safari and coming upon a group of less than twenty animals. Write a story that tells what the animals are doing. Involve groups of animals in at least three different activities. Write a number sentence and draw a picture to illustrate your story.

Seeing numbers as combinations of smaller quantities is an important basic skill for developing children's facility with arithmetic. In this problem, students break a number into at least three parts and record how the parts are combined to form a total. Children approach the problem in different ways, but I've found they often decide on the total number of animals first, remove an amount from the total by assigning a group of animals to an activity, then compare the results to the original total to find out how many animals are left, and finally break the remaining amount into two smaller parts. In the end, children have to recheck all the parts to be sure they have the correct total.

This sometimes requires them to go back and adjust one or more of the parts.

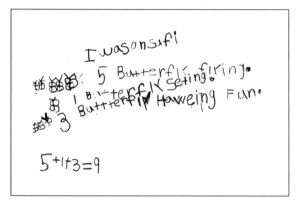

▲▲▲▲▲▲**Figure 19** *Crystal needed a small number to keep track of.*

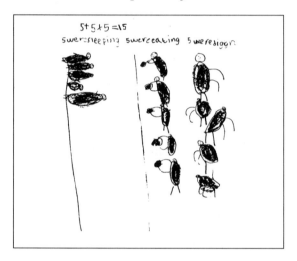

▲▲▲▲▲▲**Figure 20** *Rick split his meerkats into groups of five.*

▲▲▲▲▲▲**Figure 18** *Chanell started with two ostriches, added five, then eight more to make fifteen.*

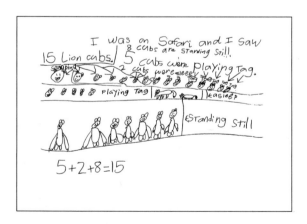

▲▲▲▲▲▲**Figure 21** *Kyle started with eight lion cubs, and split the remaining seven into groups of five and two.*

Flowers in a Flat

PROMPT

A flat of flowers holds six containers of plants, and each container holds six flower plants. How many flower plants fill a flat?

This problem grew out of a classroom situation in which we were planting flowers and needed to know how many plants were in a flat of flowers. This assessment models how to use a classroom situation with which children are familiar to evaluate students' arithmetic problem-solving skills. This particular situation most likely won't mirror one that occurs in your classroom; the situation doesn't even occur each year in my class. However, the problem is still one that I've found to be accessible to first graders and useful as an assessment. As with all problem-solving situations, students can solve this problem by drawing pictures and counting or by using other numerical strategies.

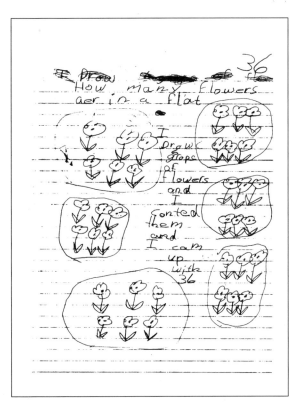

▲▲▲▲▲▲**Figure 23** *Belinda drew pictures and counted.*

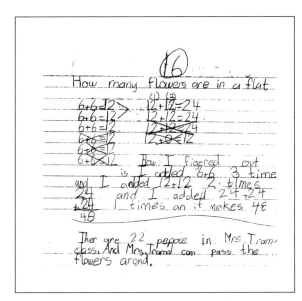

▲▲▲▲▲▲**Figure 22** *Samantha almost got carried away with adding 6 + 6, but her written explanation helped her find some of the unneeded arithmetic. However, she still solved the problem incorrectly. As an extension, I asked Samantha whether one flat of flowers would be enough for all the students in the class next door.*

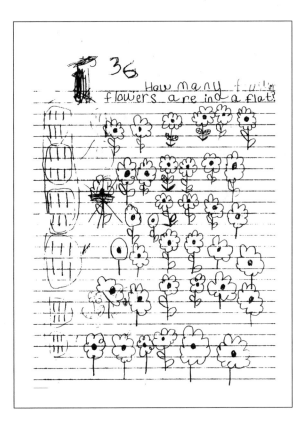

▲▲▲▲▲▲**Figure 24** *Akeem drew flowers and then drew tallies to check himself.*

Assessments 143

Lunch Count

PROMPT

For today's lunch count I'm giving you a chart to fill out. We'll count how many children would like a school sack lunch or brought a lunch from home. Then you'll figure out how many children will have chicken nuggets.

This problem models how to use a regular classroom routine to assess students' arithmetic skills. On this day, the children's school lunch choices included chicken nuggets and a sack lunch. After distributing the chart to each child, we determined that no one was absent, and the children recorded a zero in the correct place. Then we took the counts for children who chose a school sack lunch and who brought a lunch from home. Finally, the children worked to figure out how many children wanted chicken nuggets. This is a two-part problem that requires students first to figure out how many children have already been counted and then to find the difference between that number and the total number of students in the class. This particular assignment required students to figure out the difference between six and twenty-one.

Children had had a good deal of prior experience with this type of problem before I assigned this assessment. When doing lunch counts, I often lead a whole-class discussion in which we figure out how many want chicken nuggets or some other choice. Then we count to check. However, to use this problem-solving experience for an assessment, I ask the children to work individually on the problem. After I collect all of the children's papers, we count those who chose chicken nuggets and discuss the strategies the children used to figure out this problem.

I wait until the second half of the year to use this sort of problem situation as an assessment. By then, children have seen many ways of thinking about this situation, and all have at least one way to solve it.

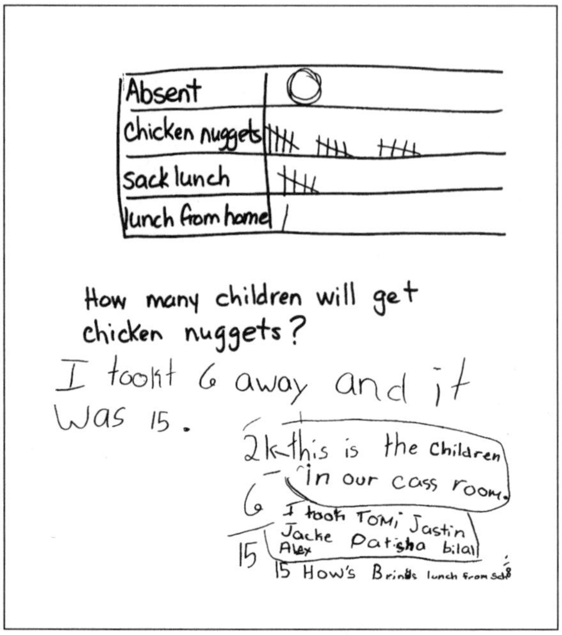

▲▲▲▲▲▲**Figure 25** *It's clear that Adrianna understood what each number represented.*

▲▲▲▲▲▲**Figure 26** *Angel filled in the missing tally marks on the chart to determine how many children were missing. He counted up from six to twenty-one.*

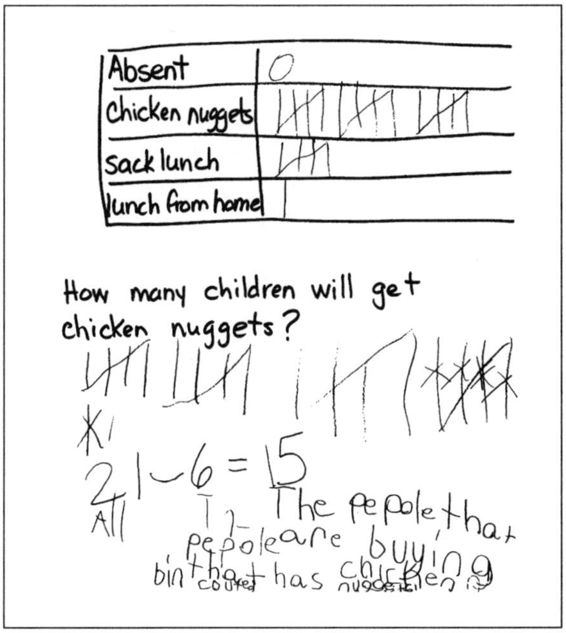

Absent | ⊘
Chicken nuggets | ||||| |||| |||| ||||
Sack lunch | |||||
Lunch from home |

How many children will get chicken nuggets?

||||| |||| |||| ||| |||| |||| ||||
|||
21 – 6 = 15
All | The pepole that pepole are buying bin couret has chicken nuggets

▲▲▲▲▲▲**Figure 27** *Bin drew twenty-one tally marks and crossed out six. His number sentence told me that he understood what the numbers stood for.*

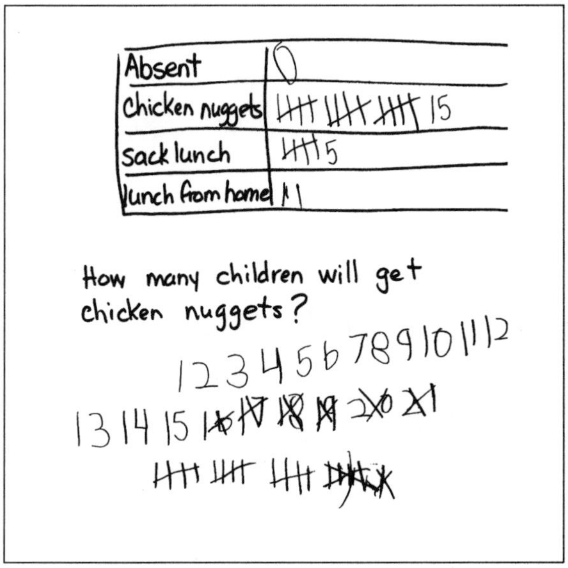

Absent | ⊘ ☆
Chicken nuggets | **15**
Sack lunch | |||| | Jo Kry Issa
Lunch from home | | Tami

How many children will get chicken nuggets?

I looked at the number chart and I Tock away it 6 and it leftd 15.

▲▲▲▲▲▲**Figure 29** *Nebala used the hundreds chart on the wall to subtract.*

Absent | ⊘
Chicken nuggets | |||| |||| |||| 15
Sack lunch | |||| 5
Lunch from home | | |

How many children will get chicken nuggets?

1 2 3 4 5 6 7 8 9 10 11 12
13 14 15 16 17 18 19 20 21
|||| |||| |||| ||||

▲▲▲▲▲▲**Figure 28** *Trey subtracted by writing out the numbers 1 to 21 and crossing out the last six.*

BLACKLINE MASTERS

One-Inch Squares
Ten Flashing Fireflies
1–100 Chart

One-Inch Squares

Ten Flashing Fireflies

1–100 Chart

1	2	3	4	5	6	7	8	9	10
11	12	13	14	15	16	17	18	19	20
21	22	23	24	25	26	27	28	29	30
31	32	33	34	35	36	37	38	39	40
41	42	43	44	45	46	47	48	49	50
51	52	53	54	55	56	57	58	59	60
61	62	63	64	65	66	67	68	69	70
71	72	73	74	75	76	77	78	79	80
81	82	83	84	85	86	87	88	89	90
91	92	93	94	95	96	97	98	99	100

INDEX

151